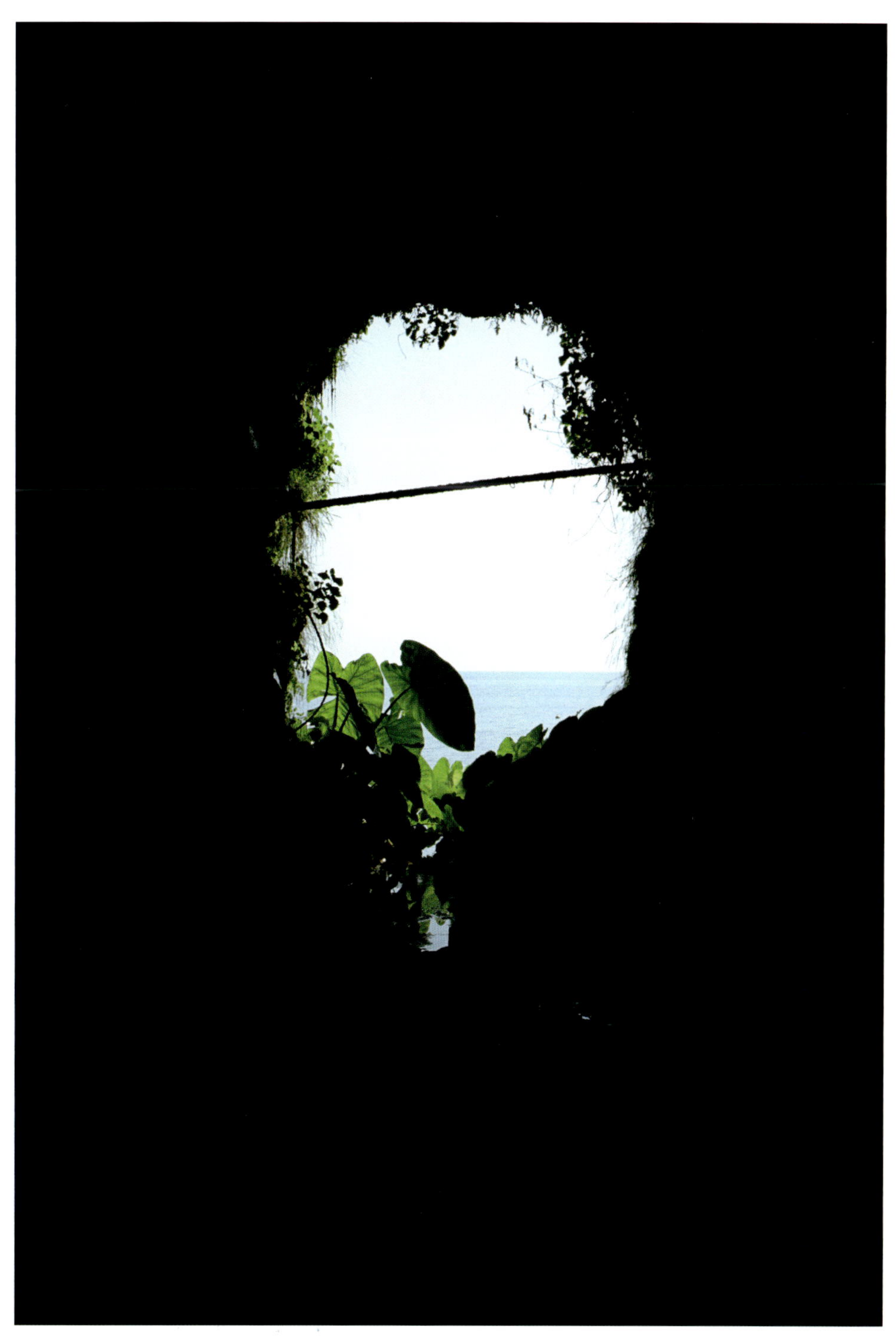

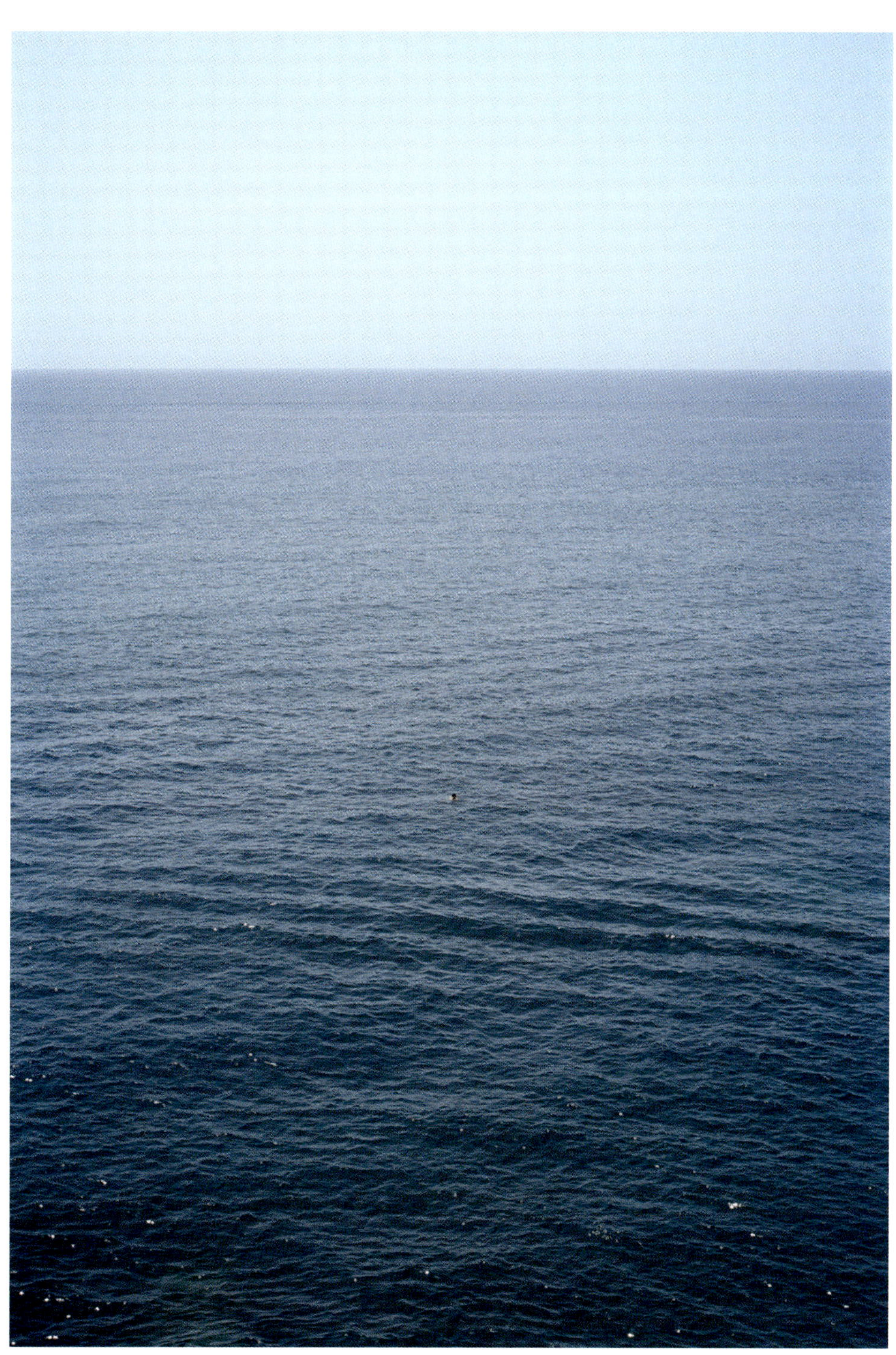

ILHA
Pedro Ramos

The Spring Press
New York, New York

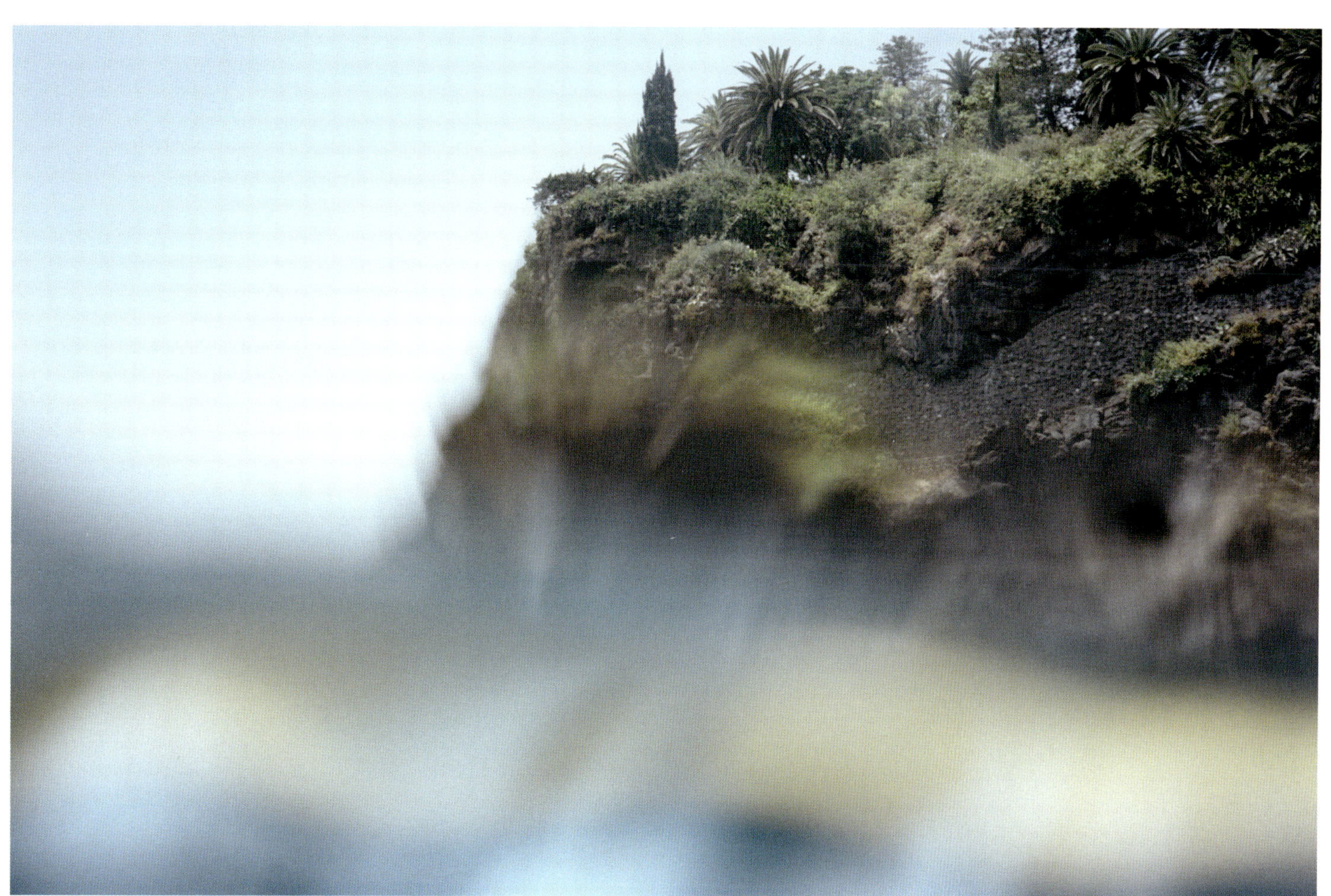

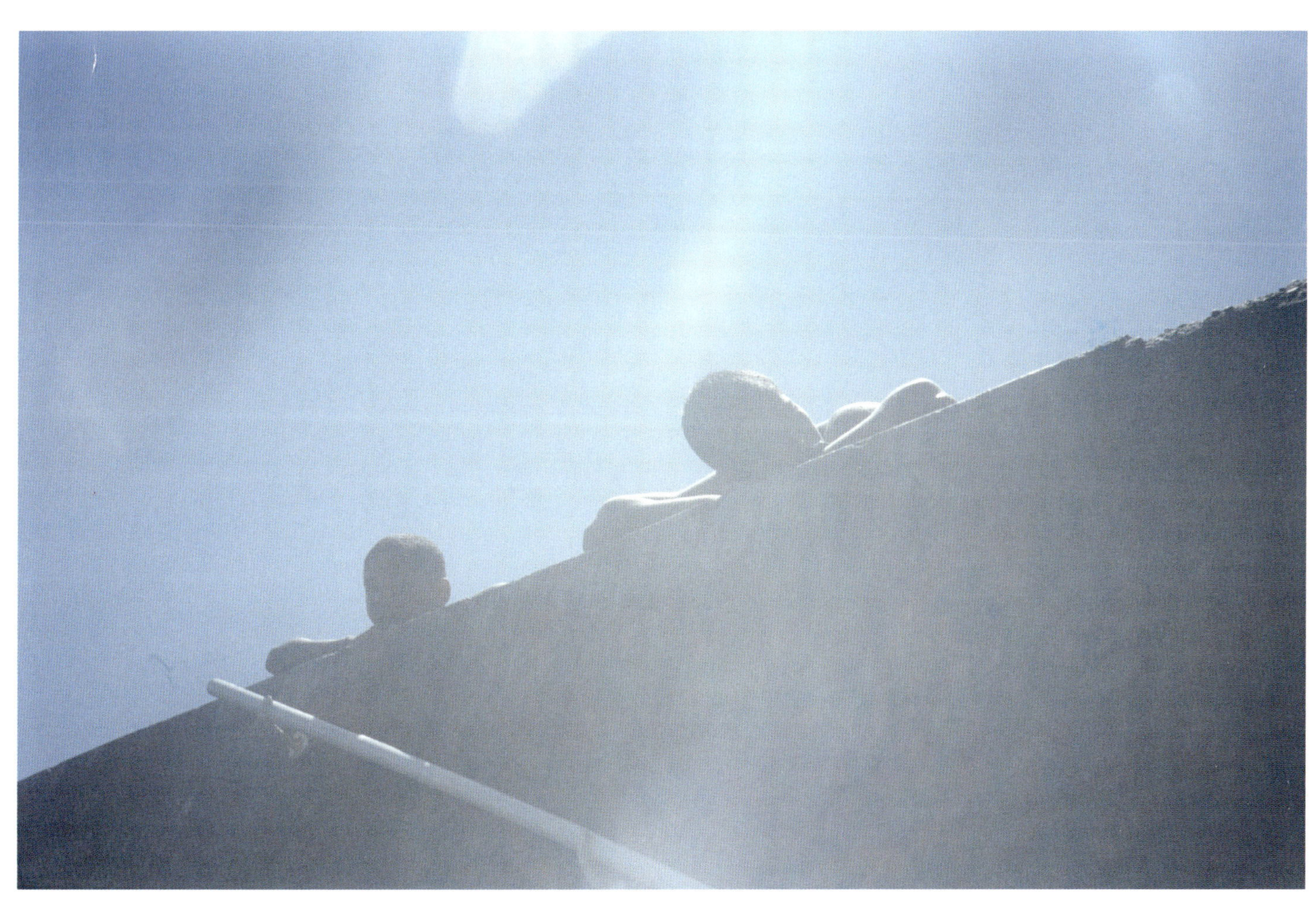

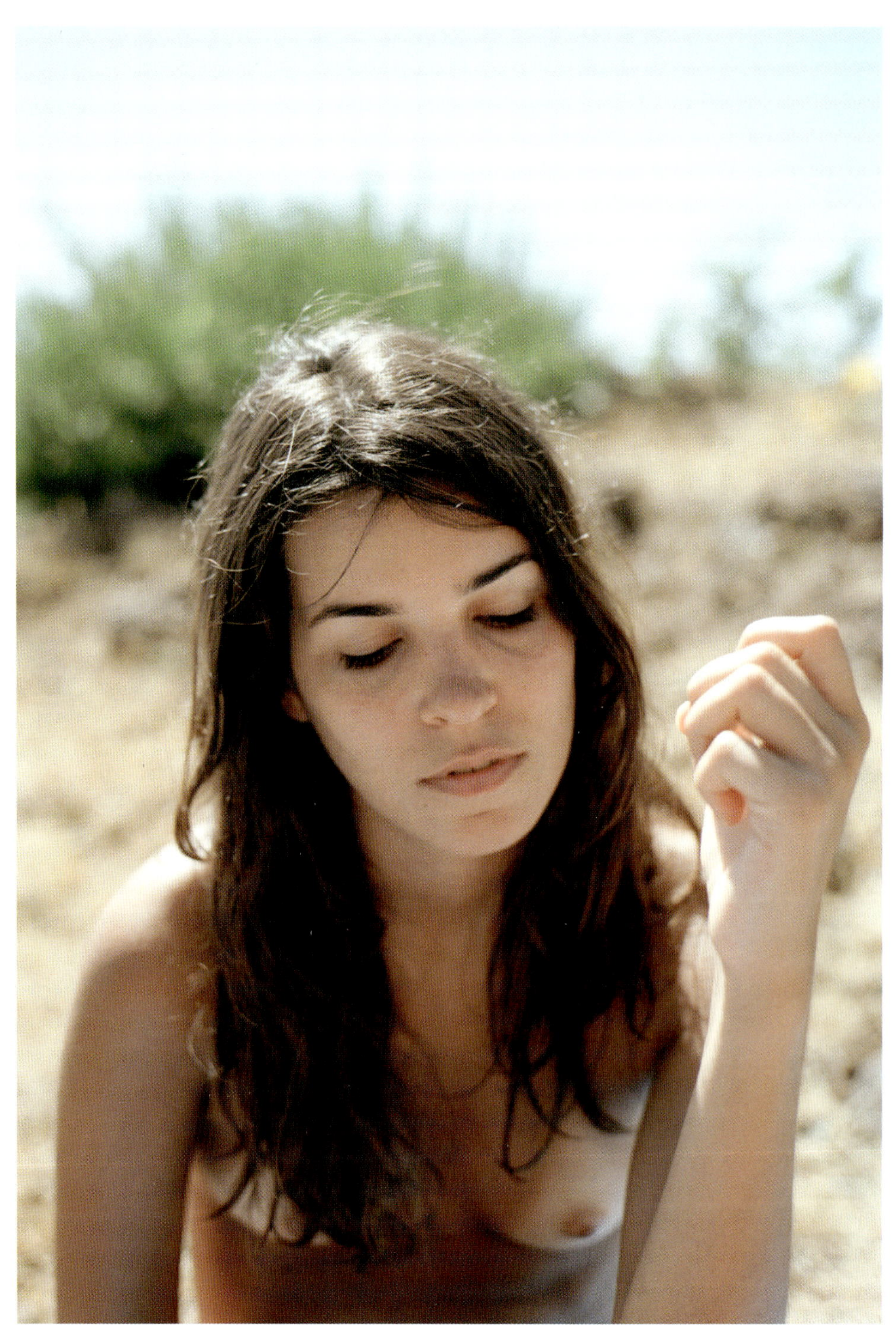

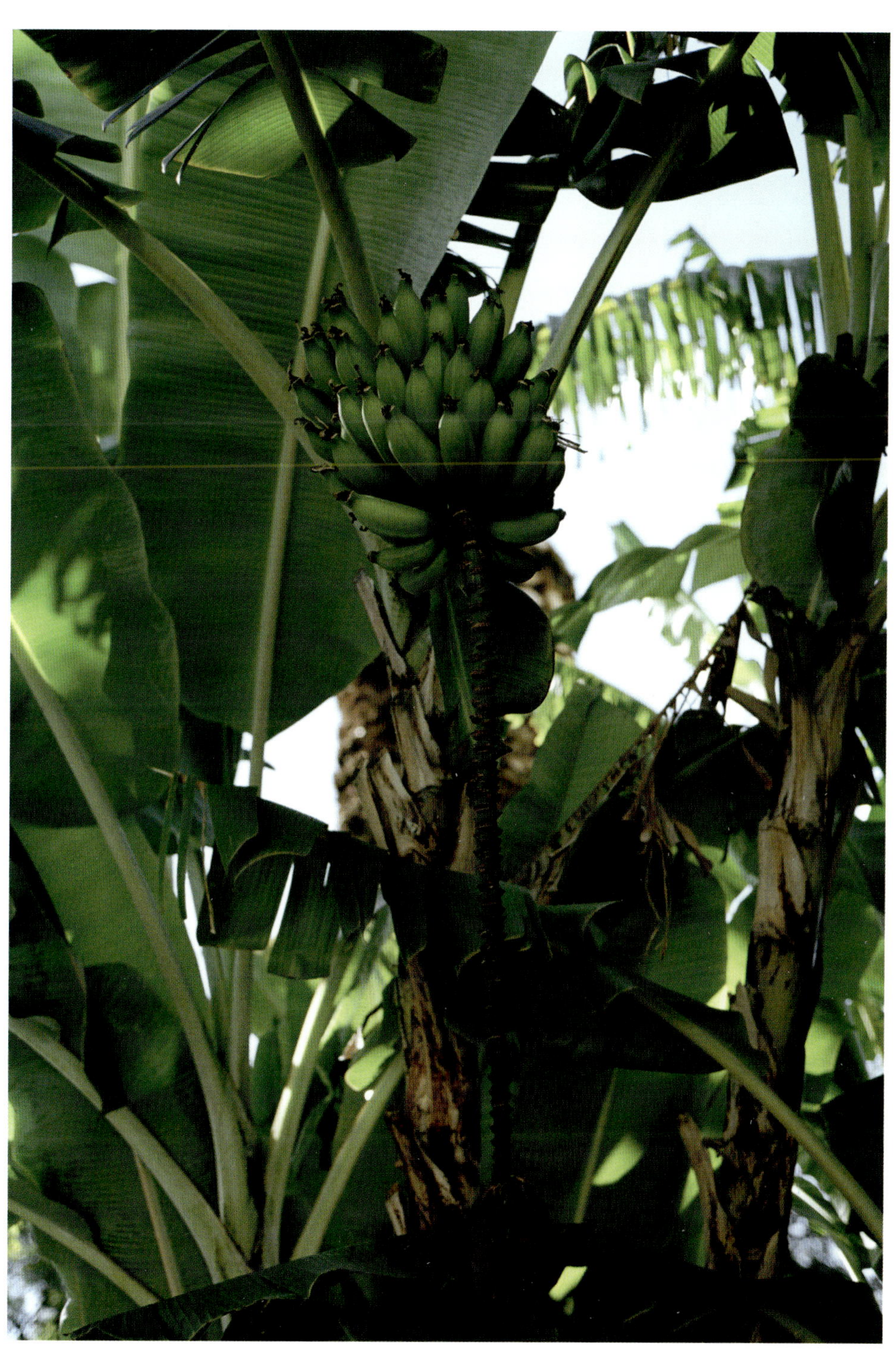

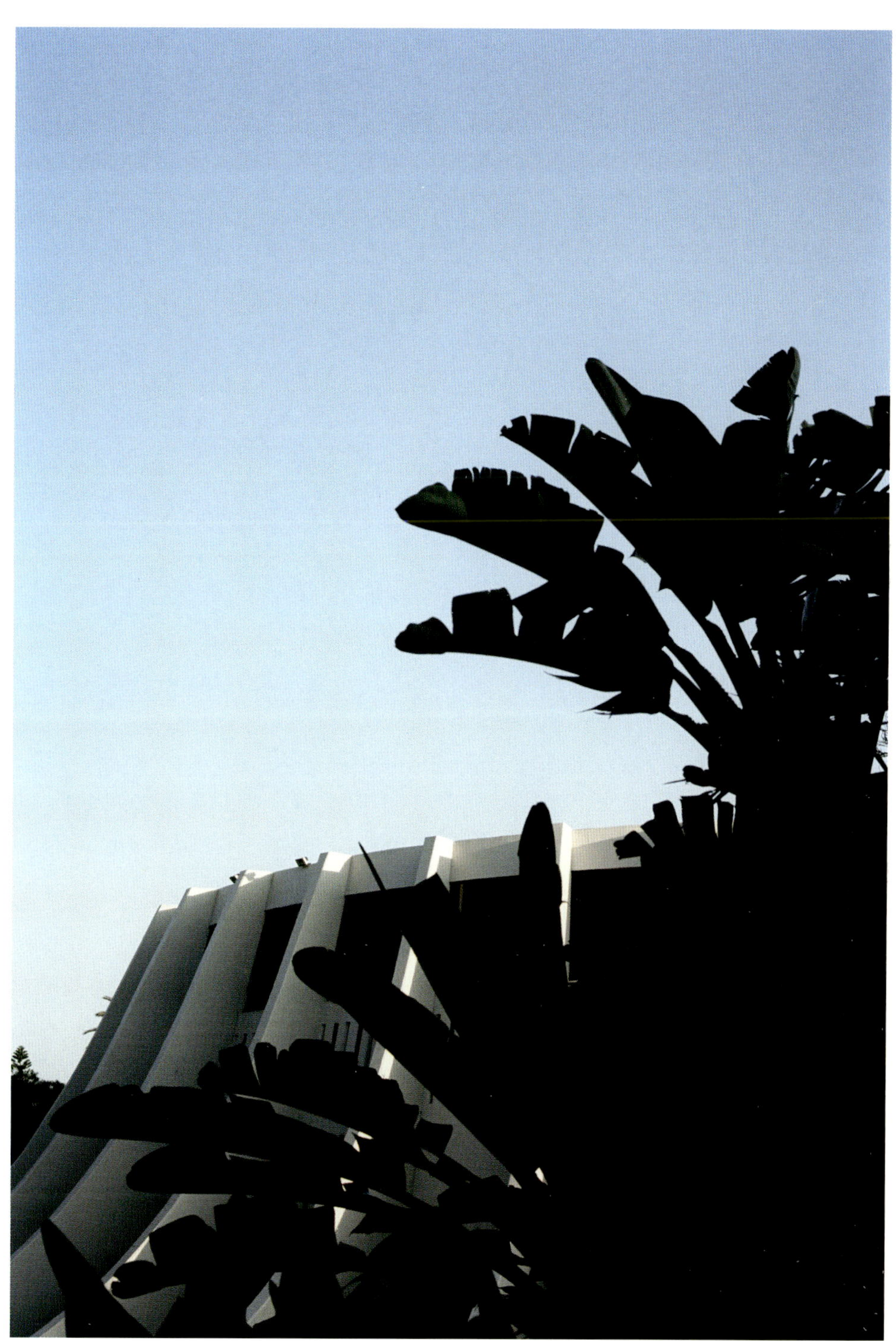

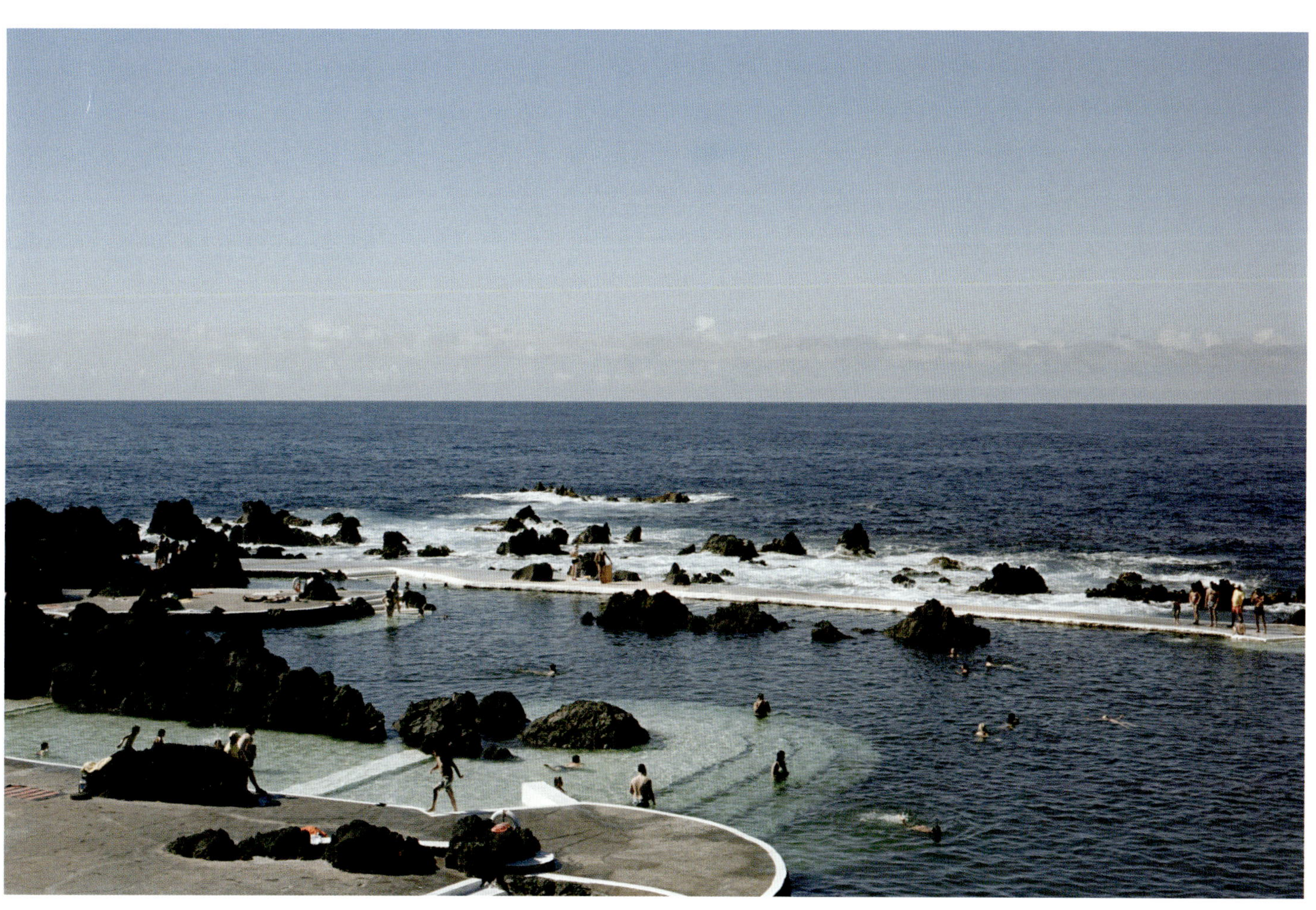

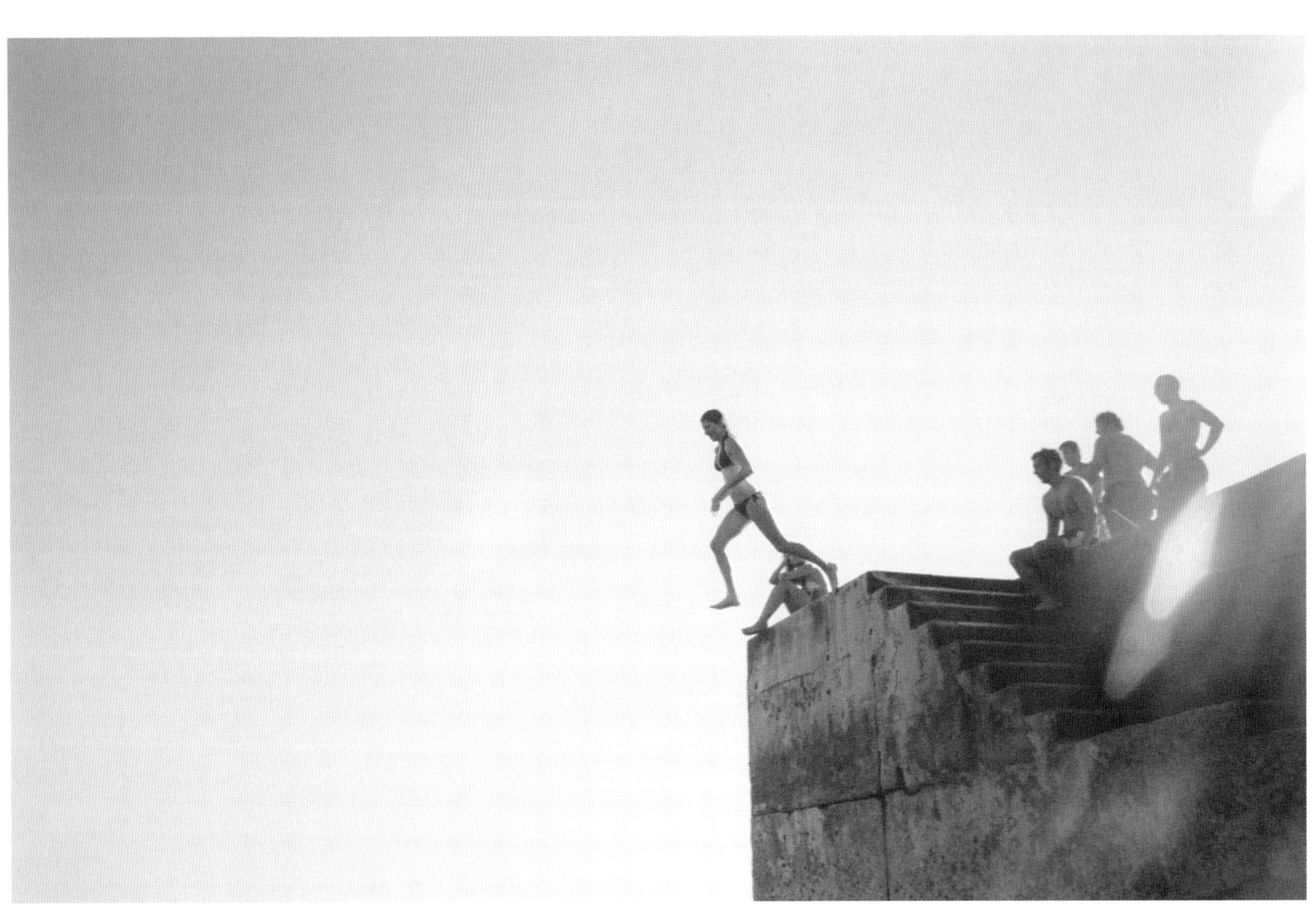

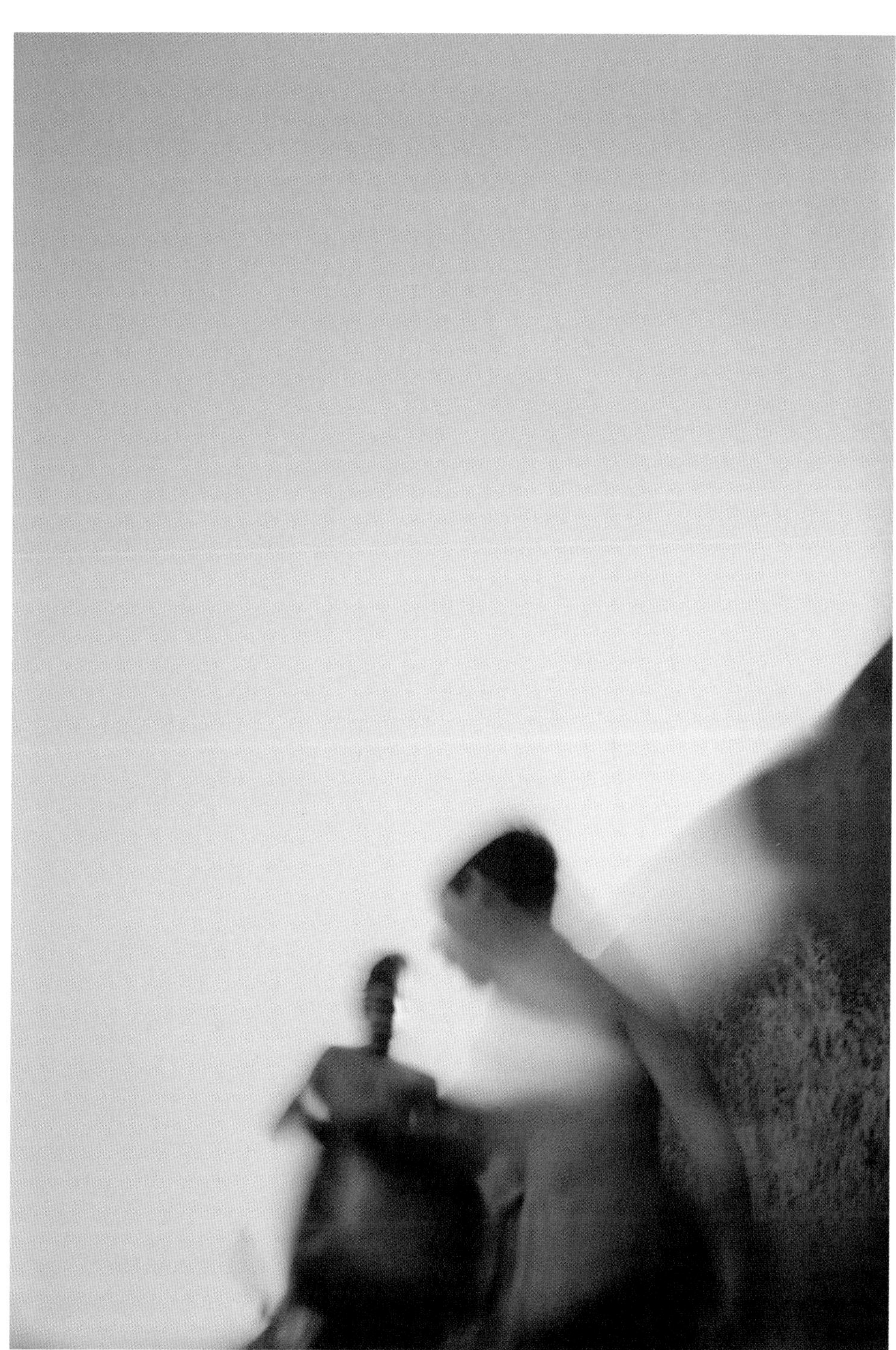

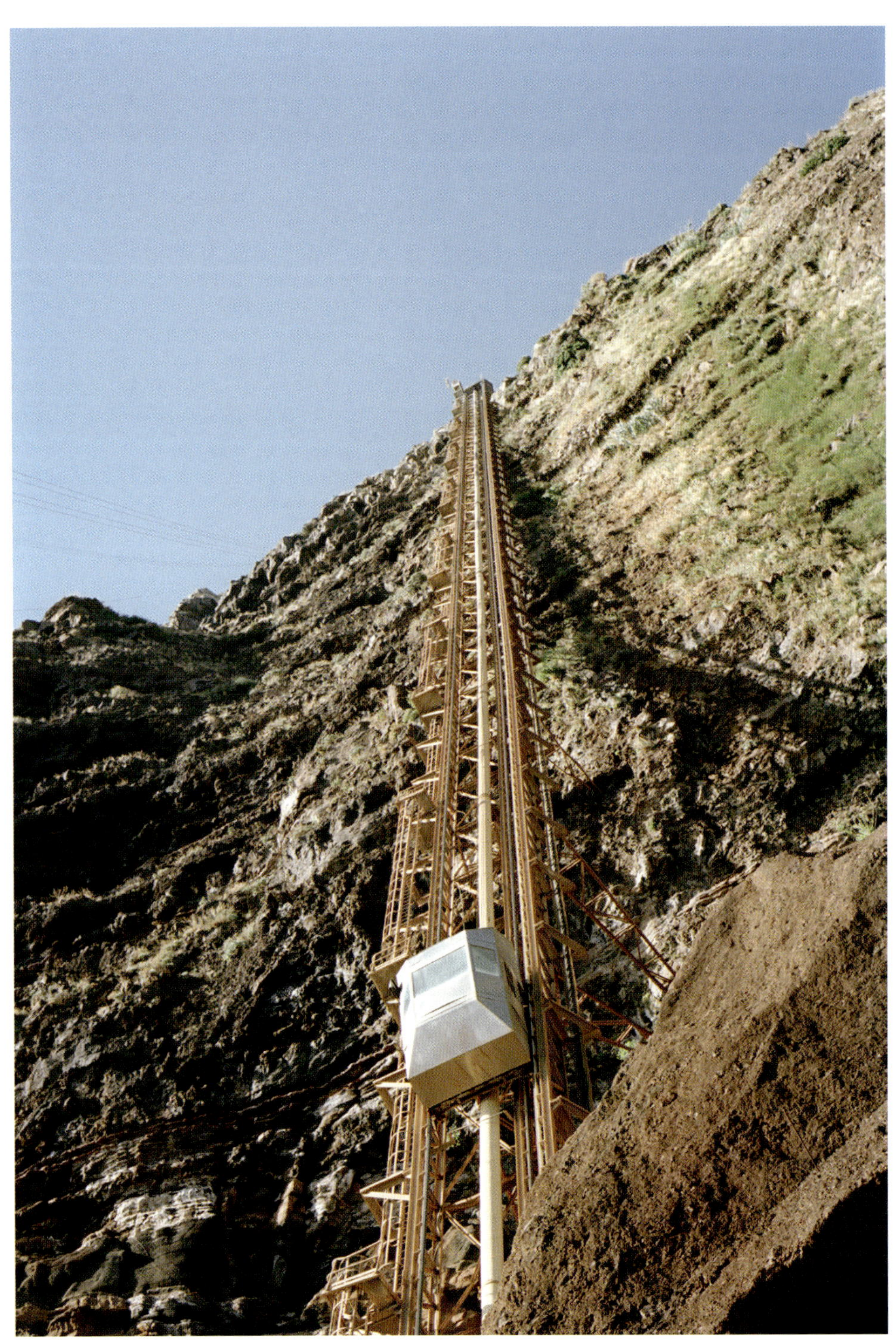

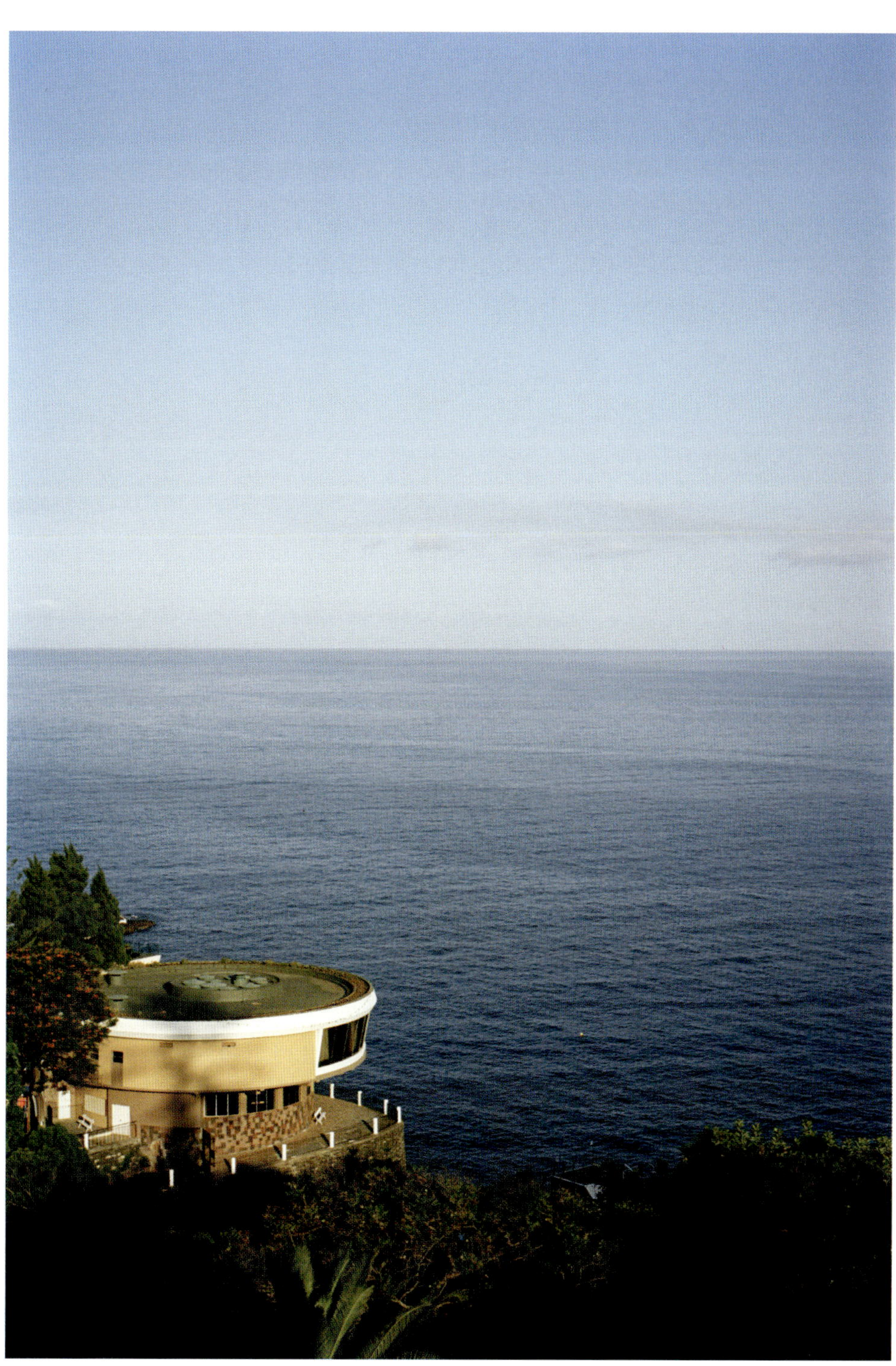

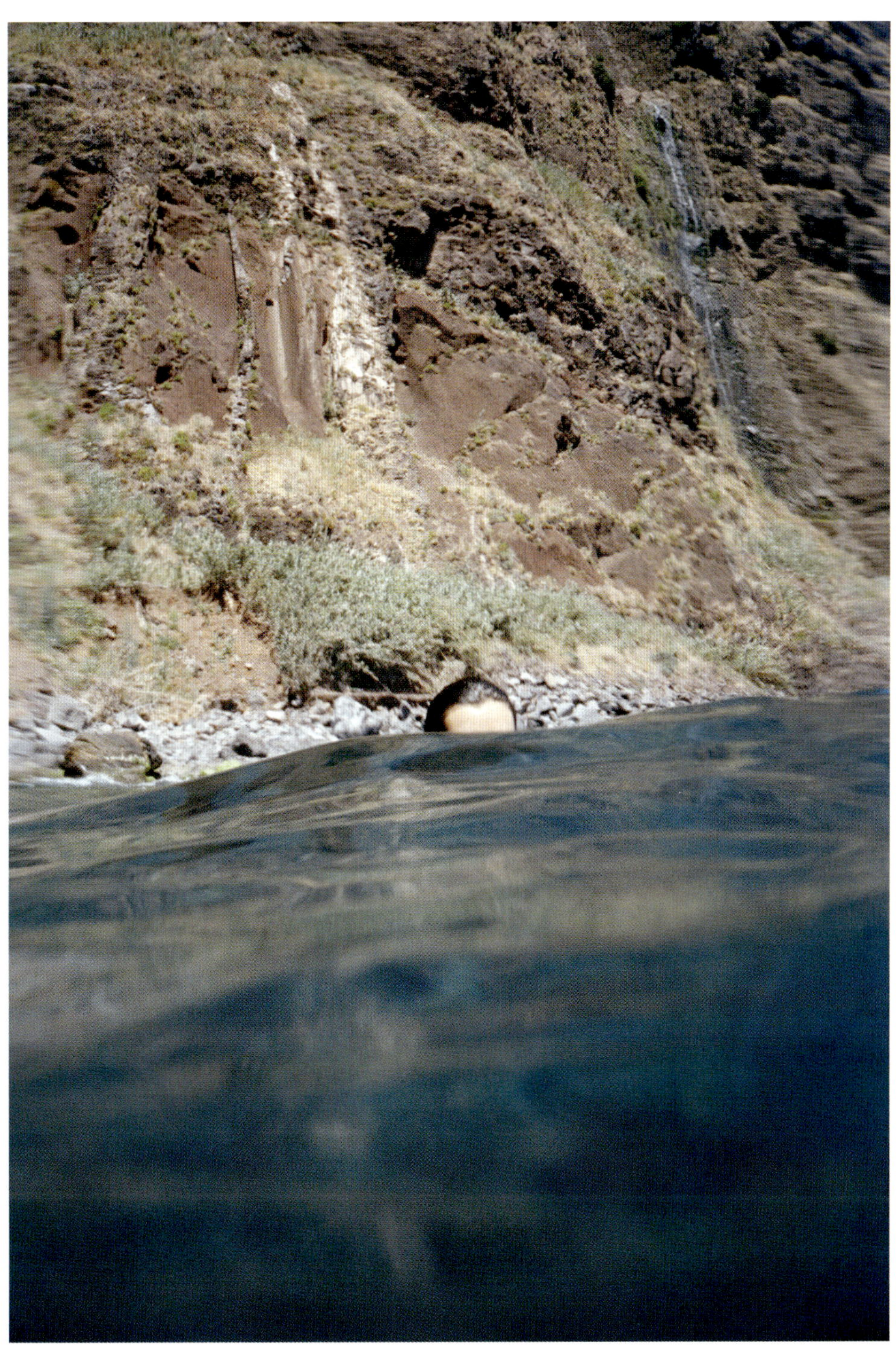

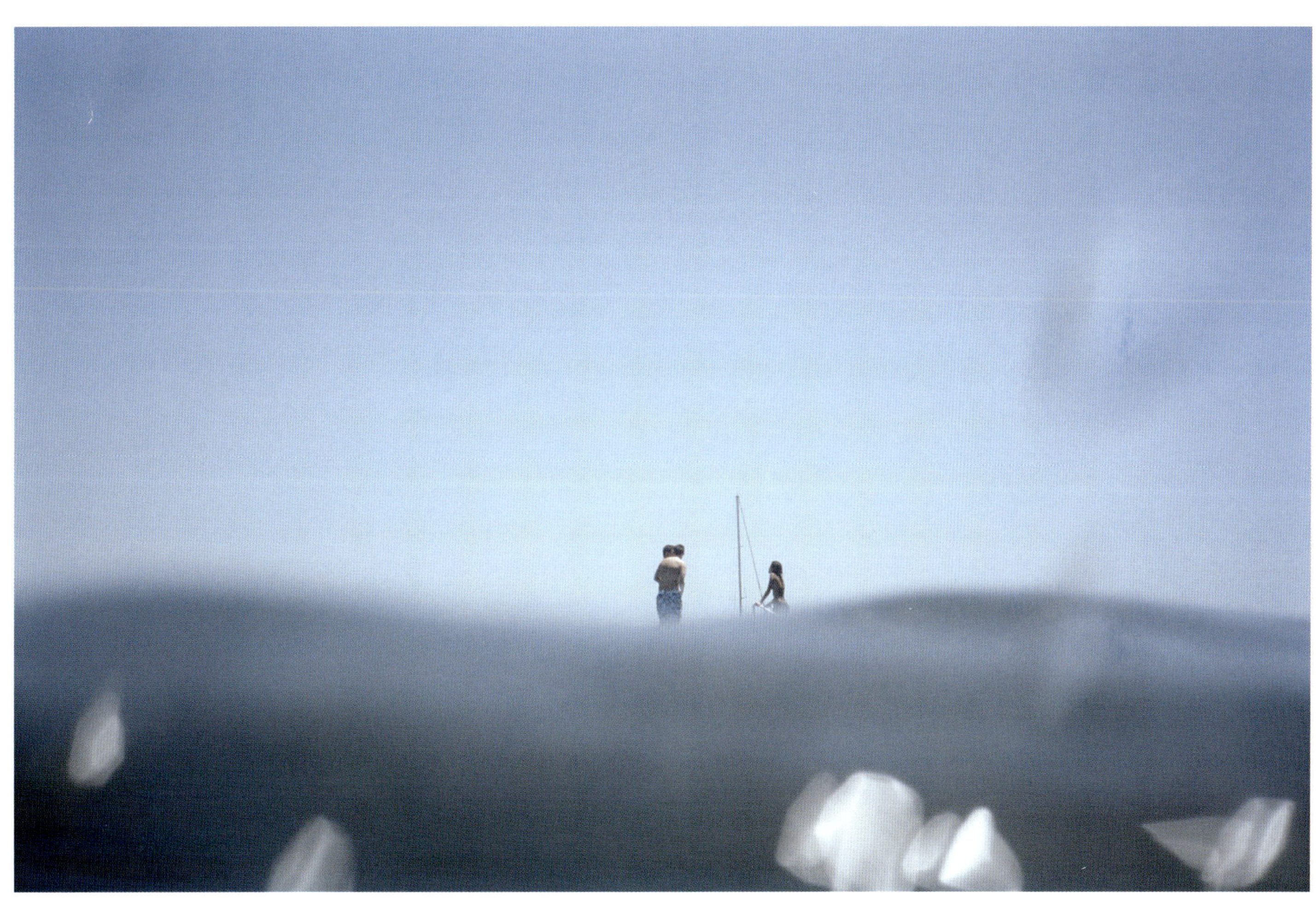

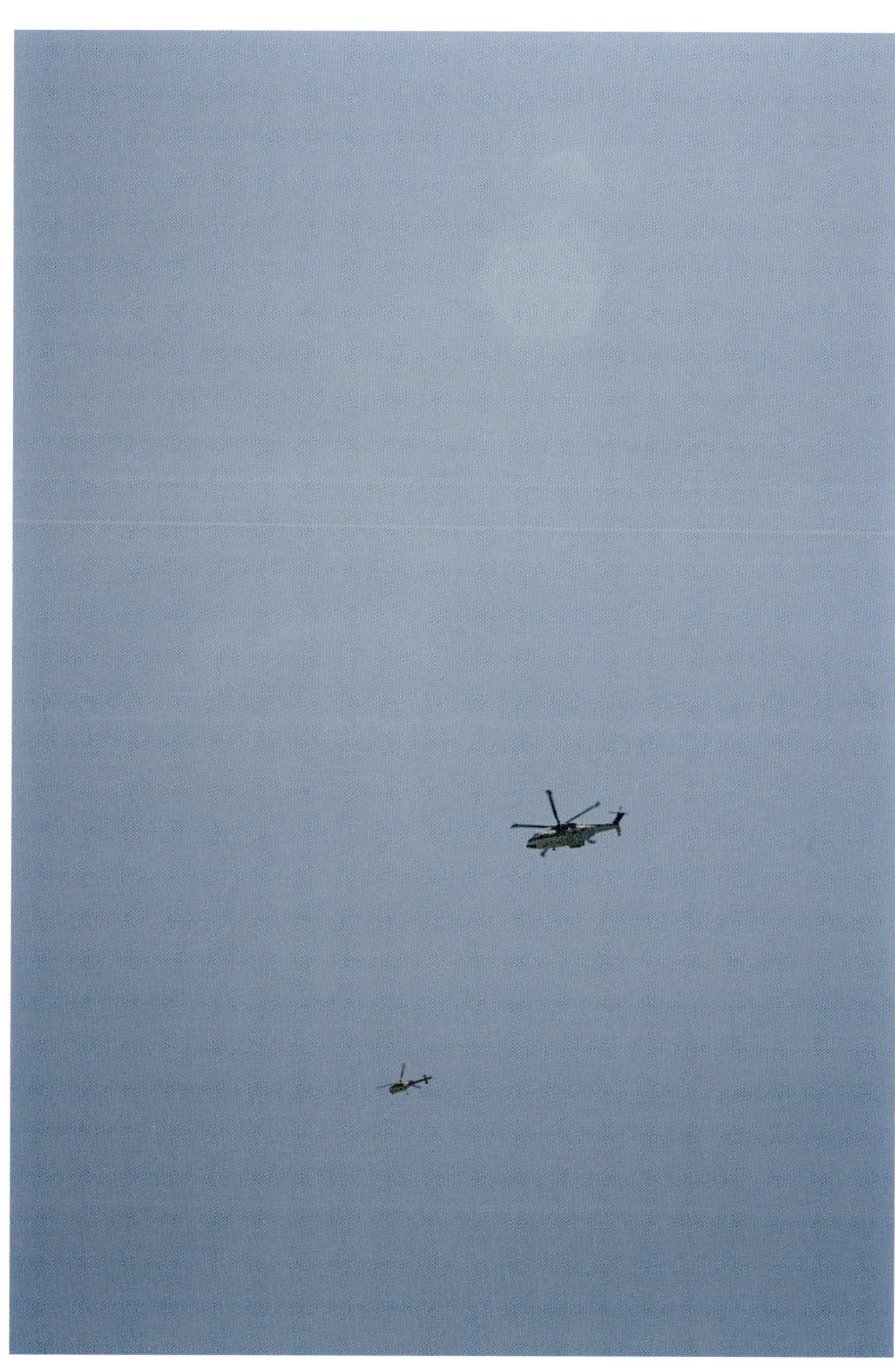

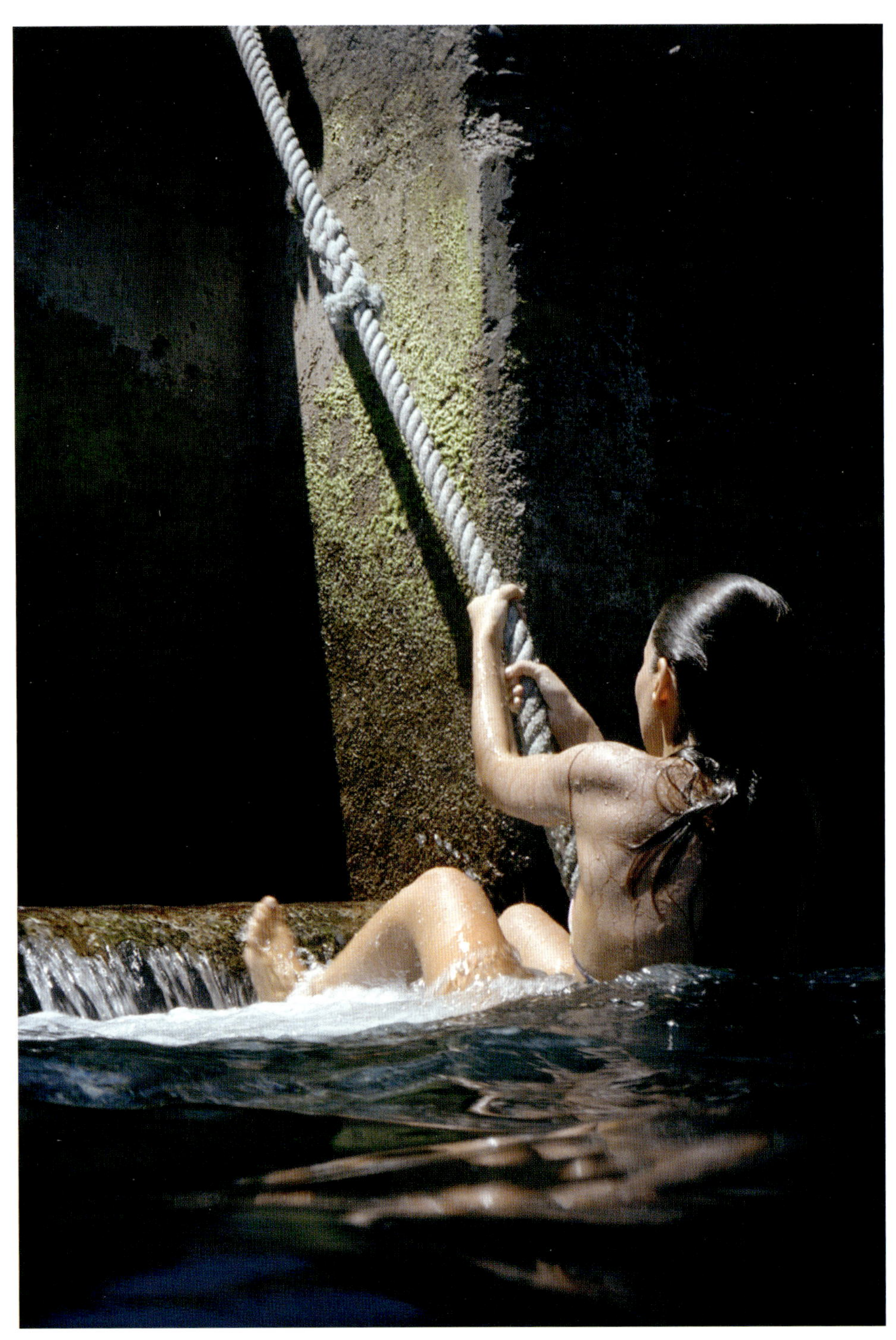

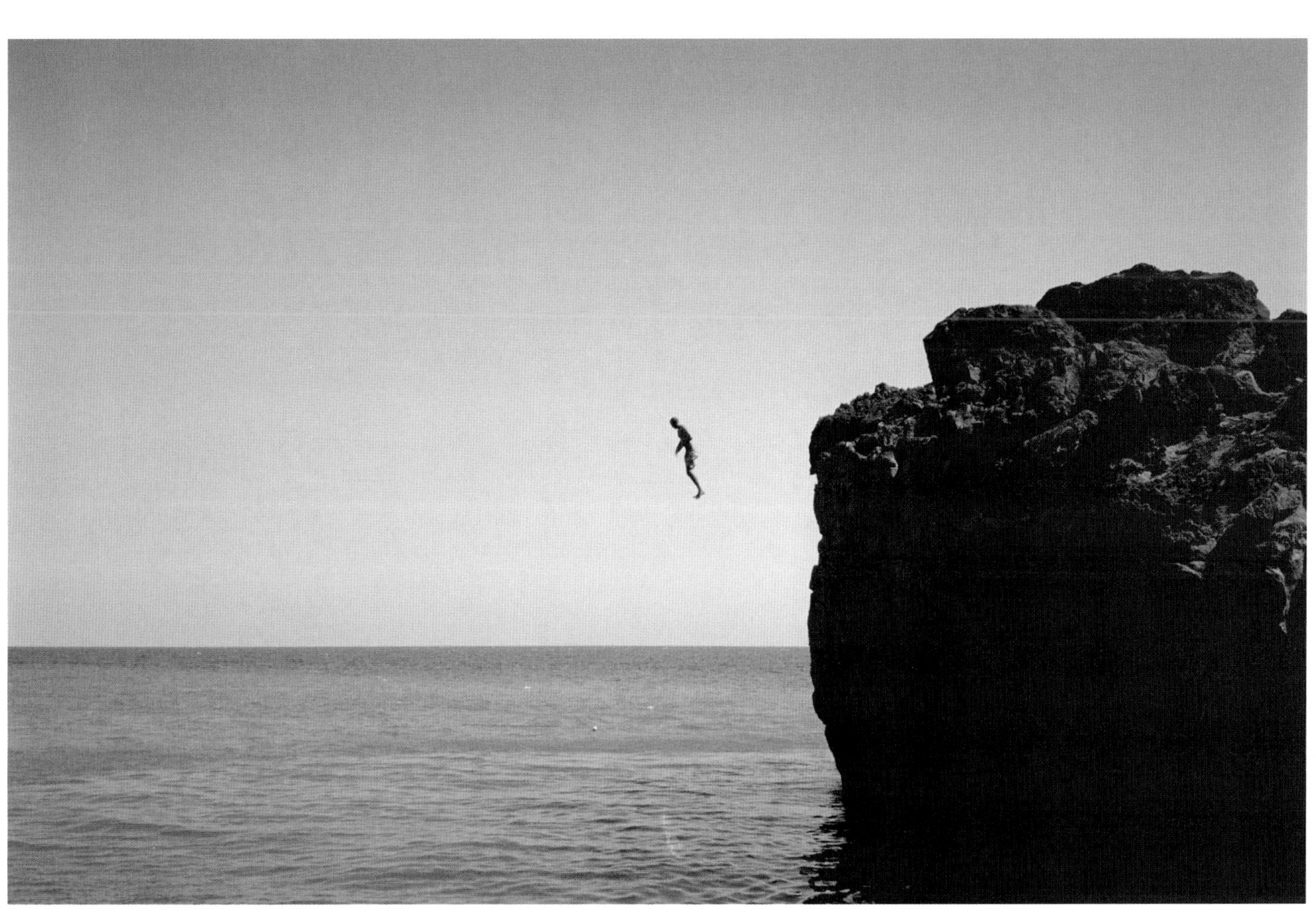

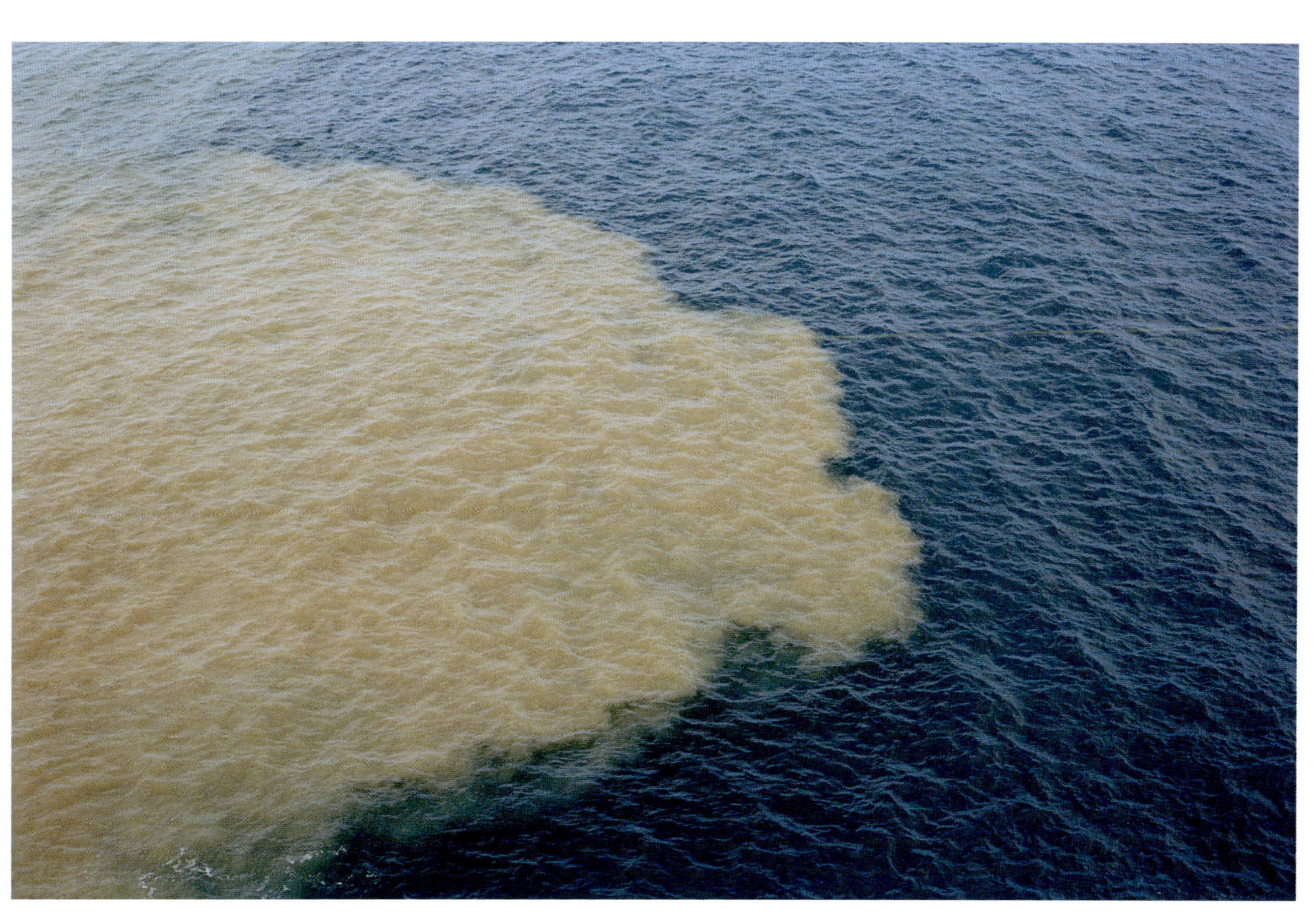

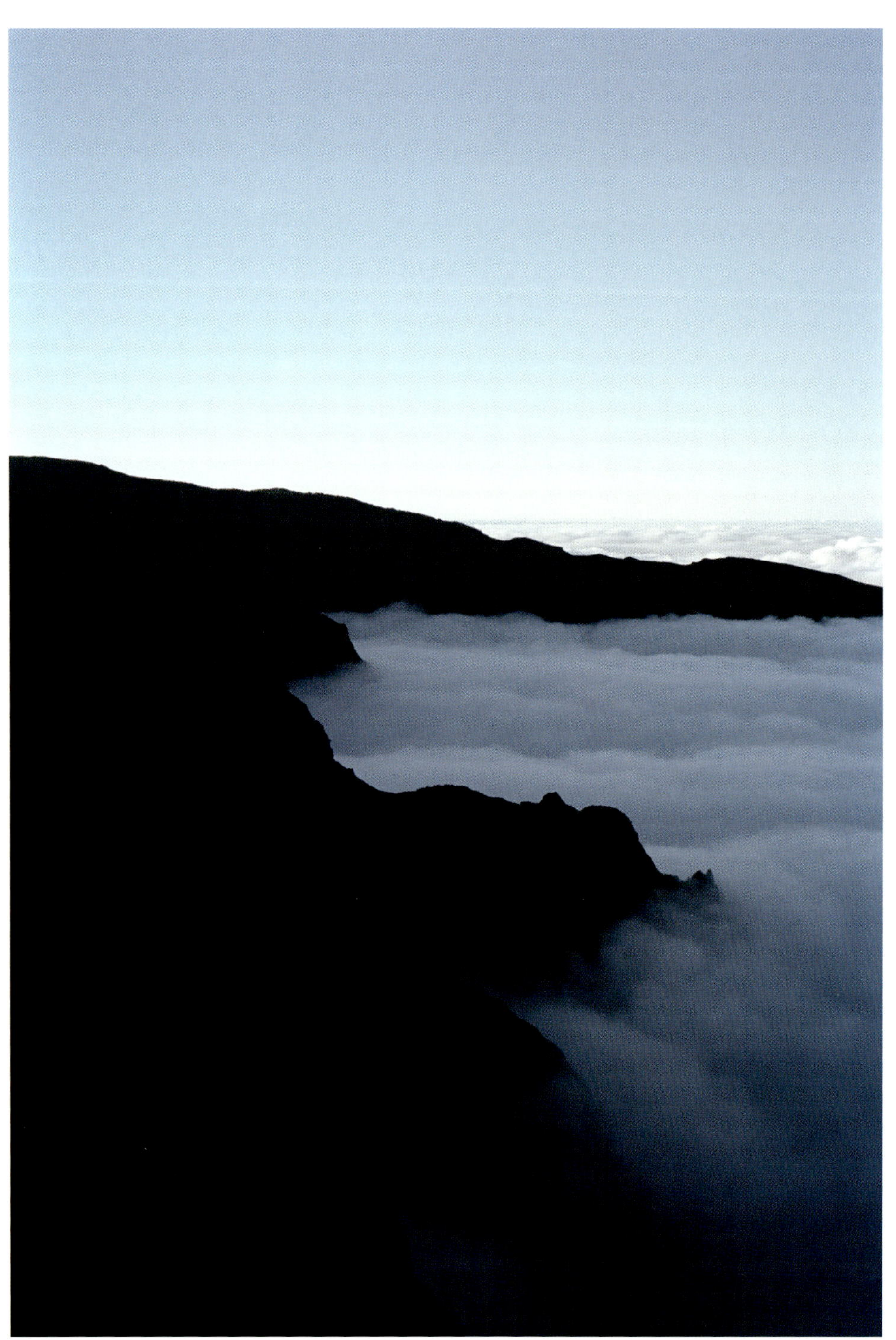

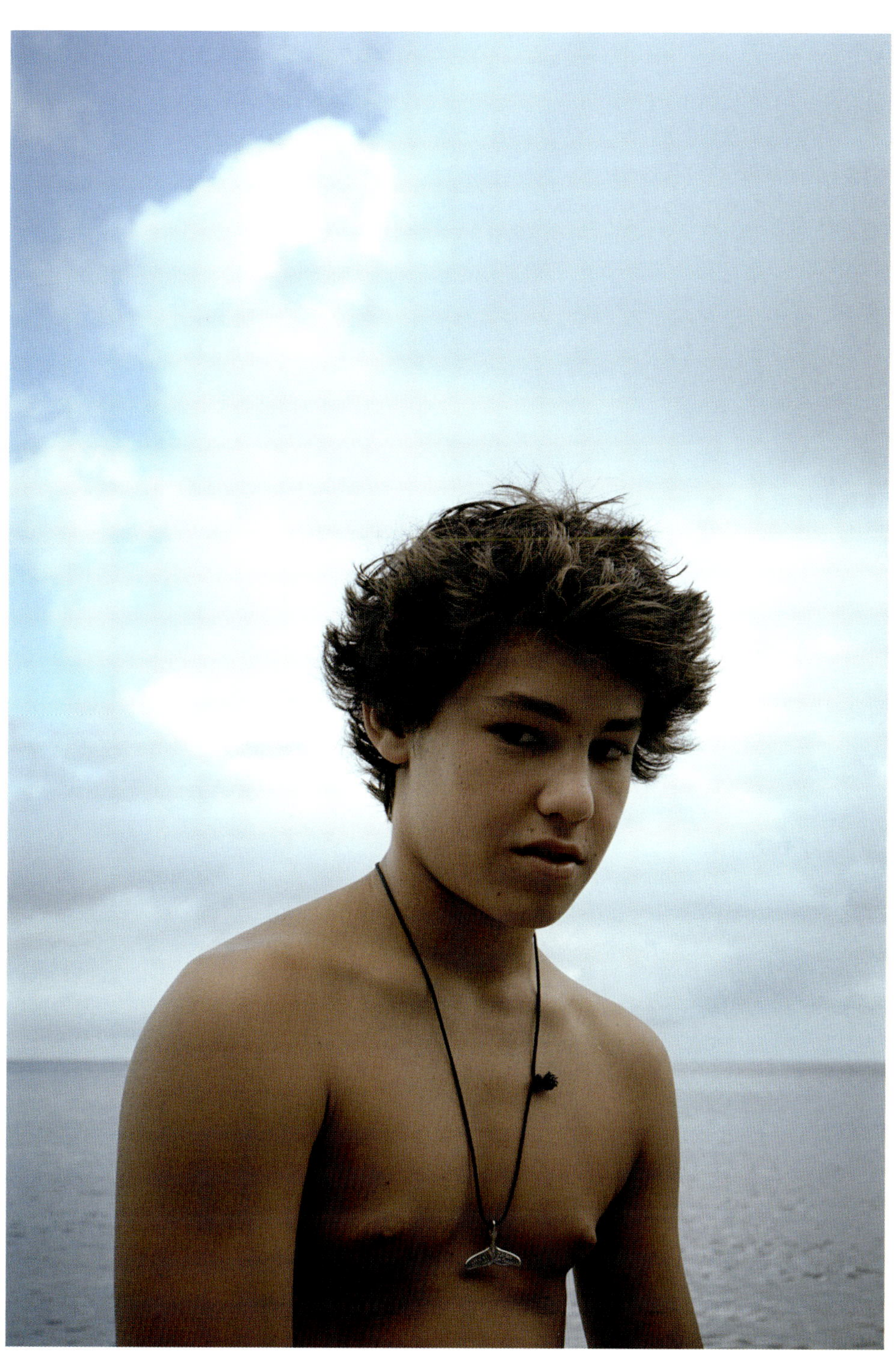

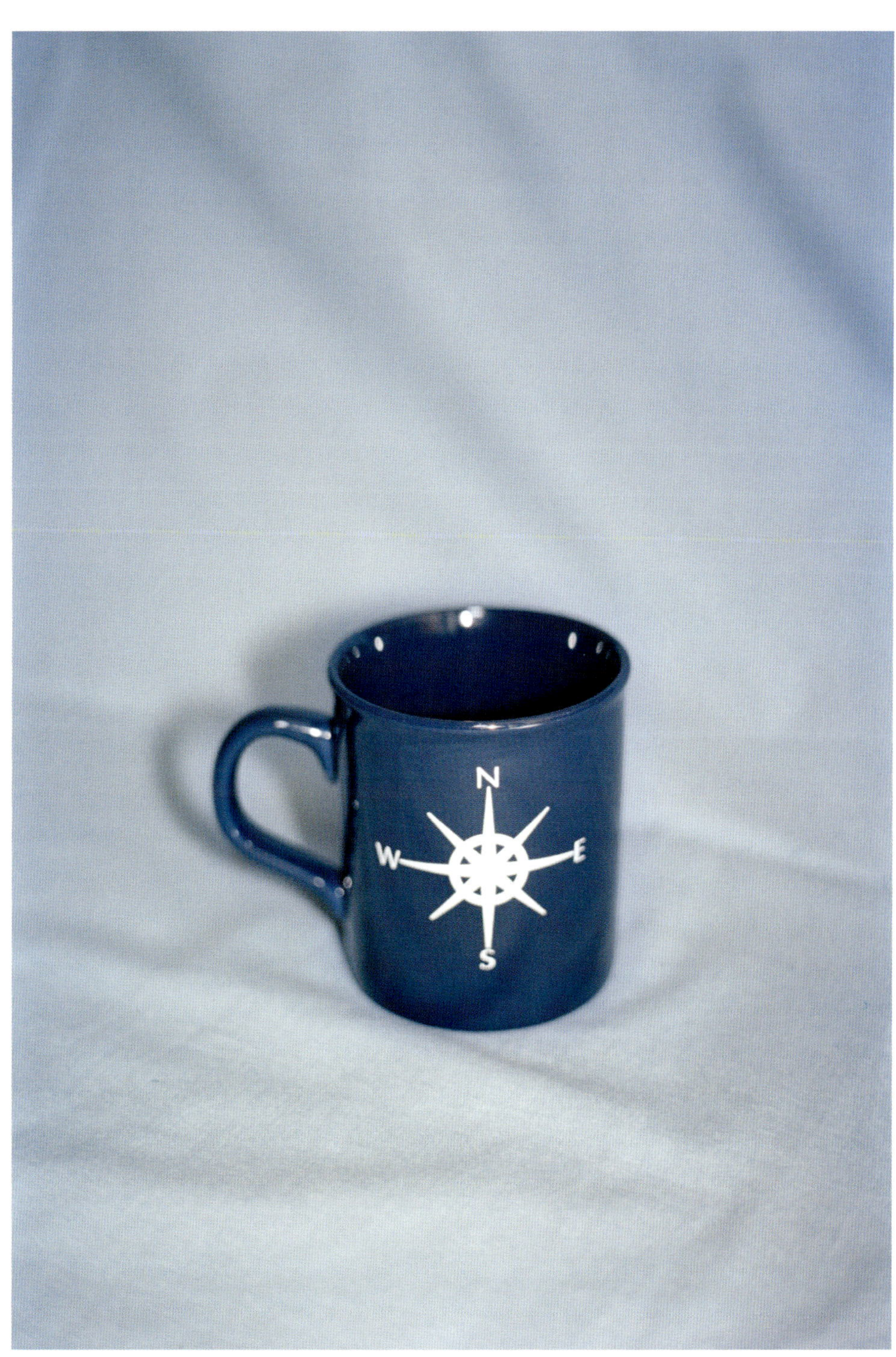
N
W
E
S

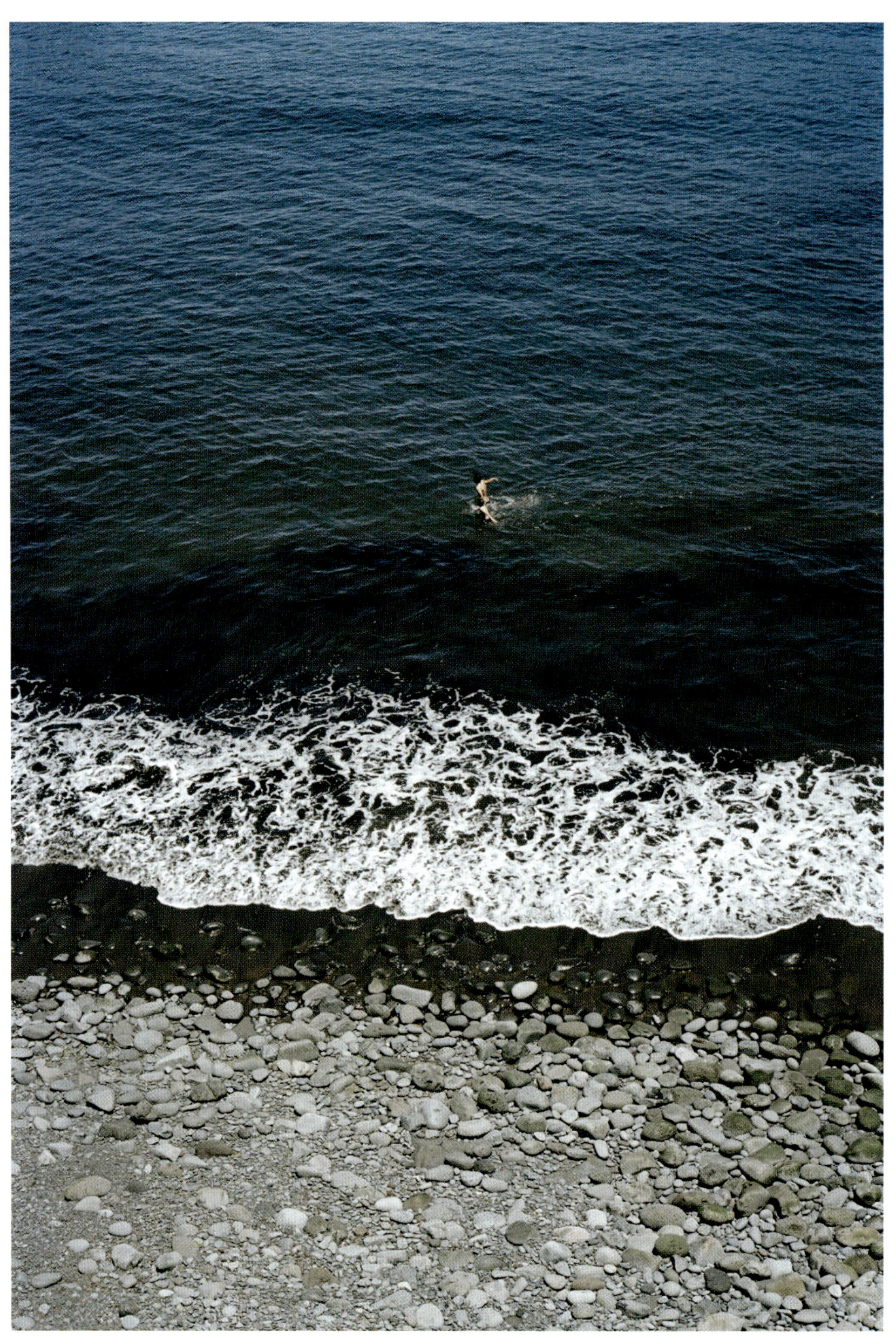

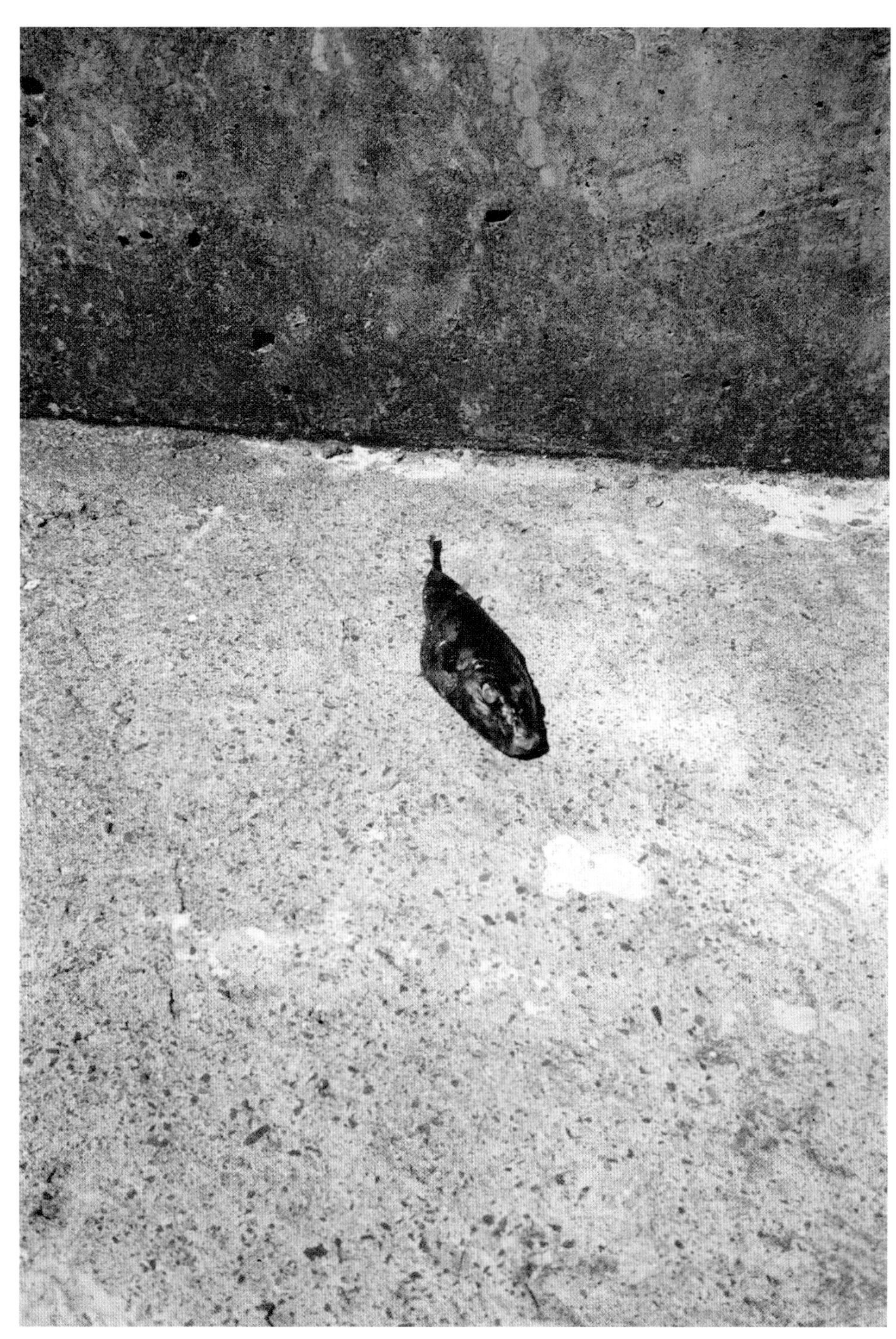

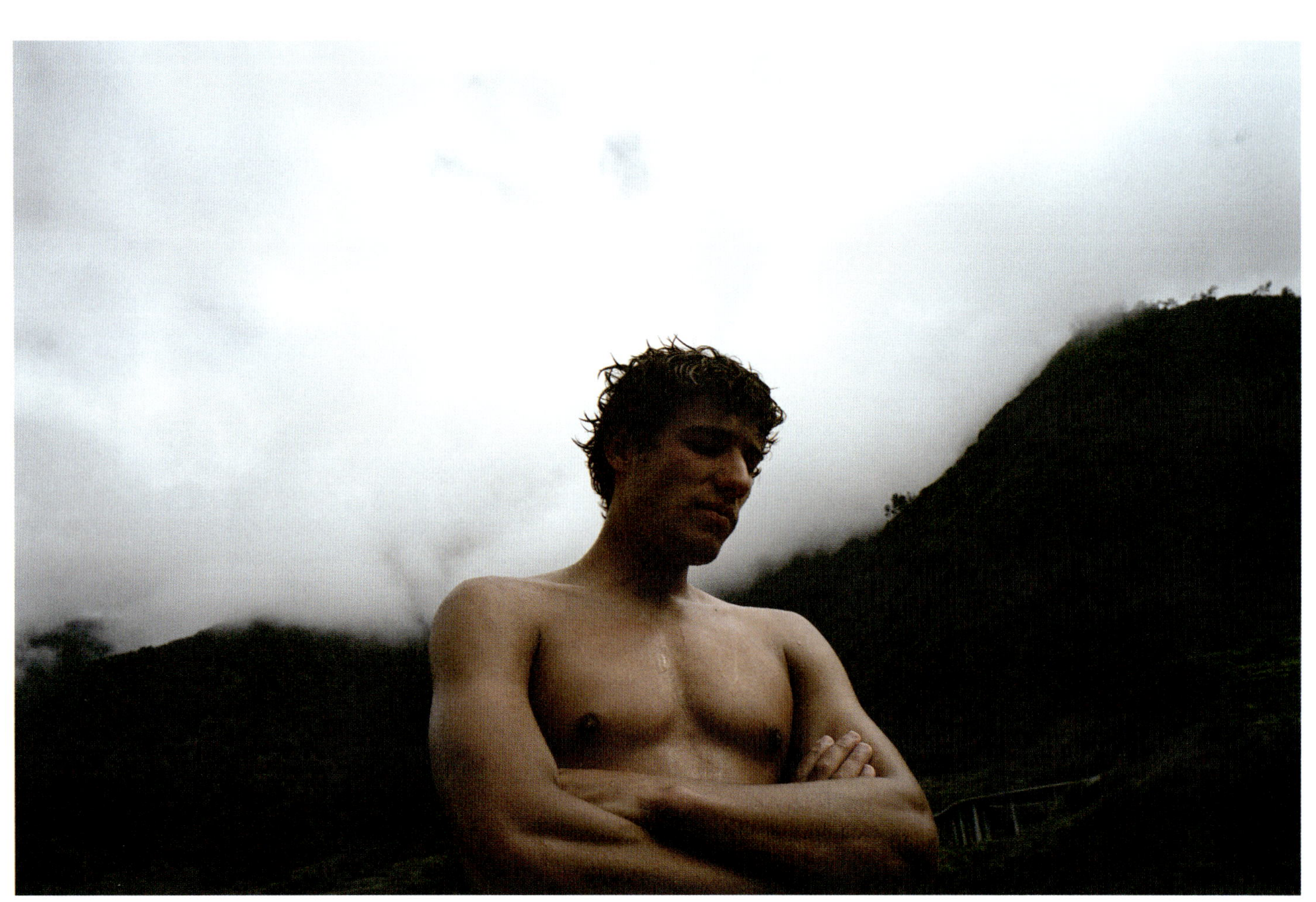

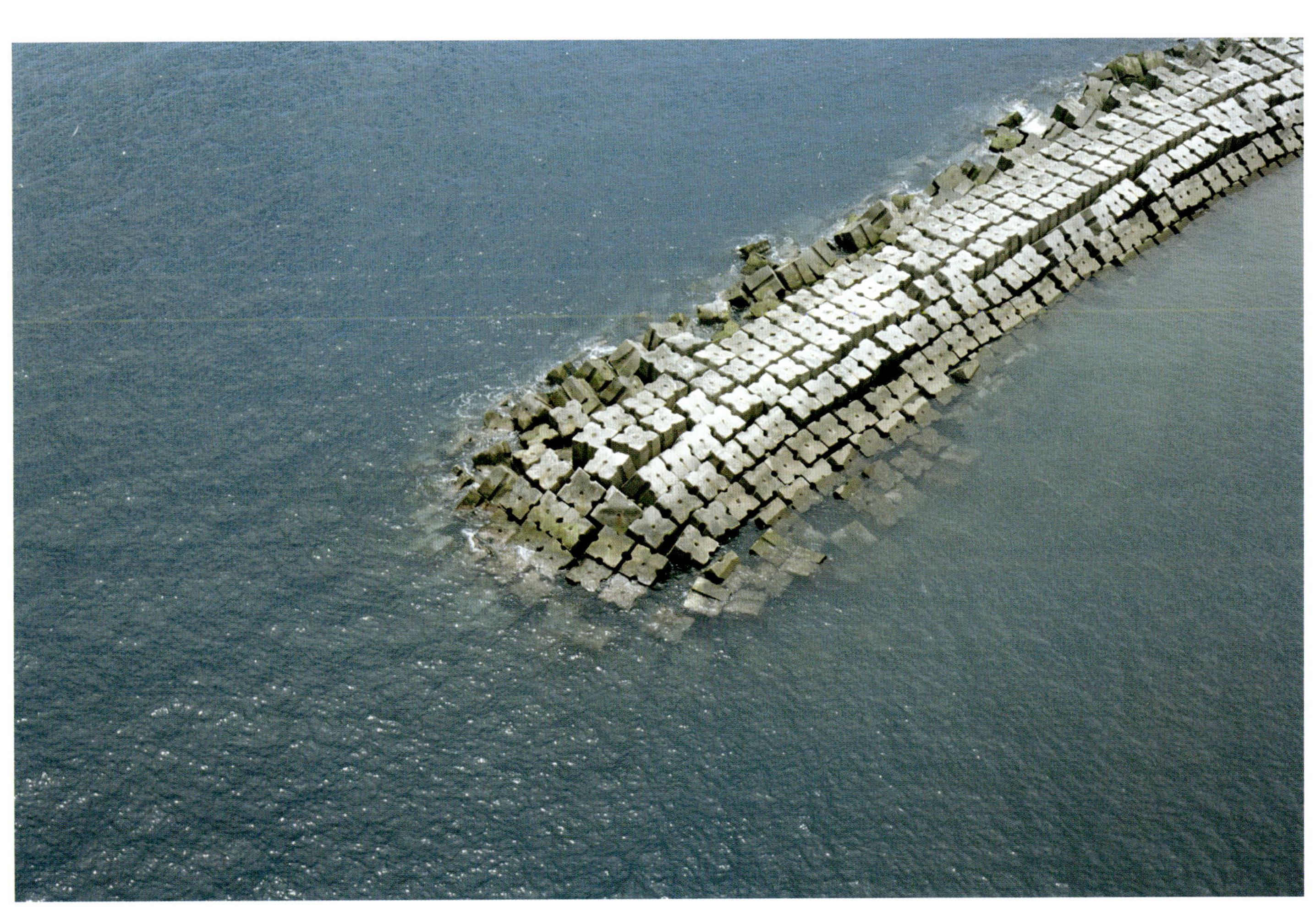

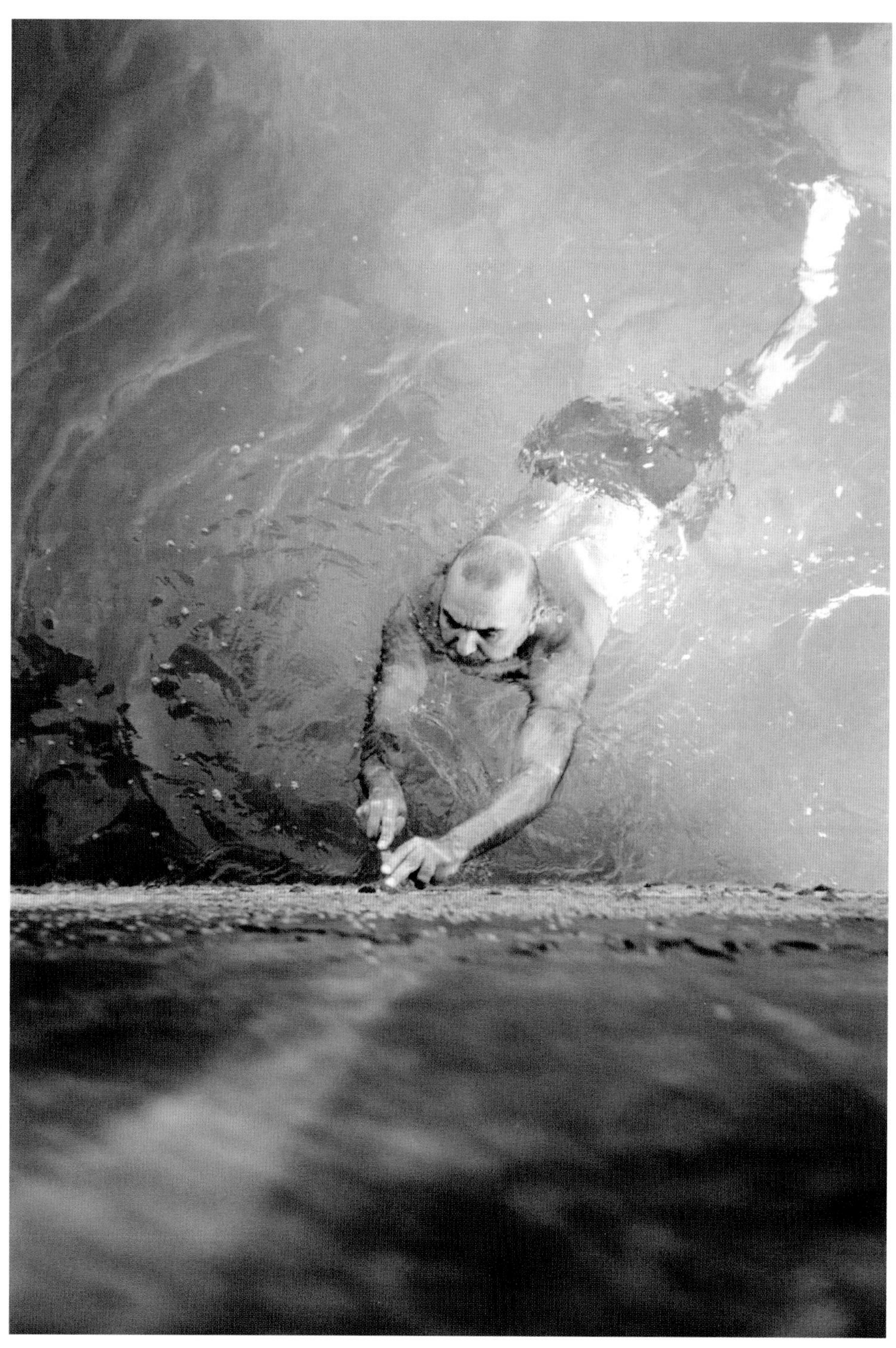

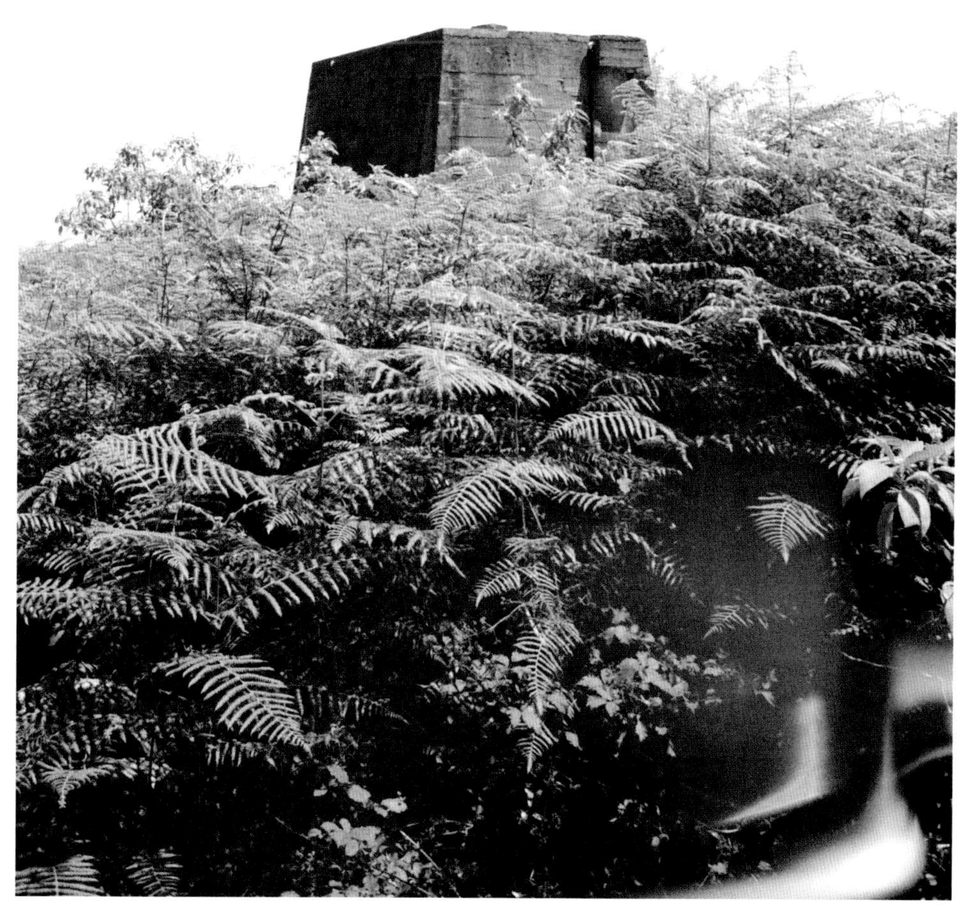

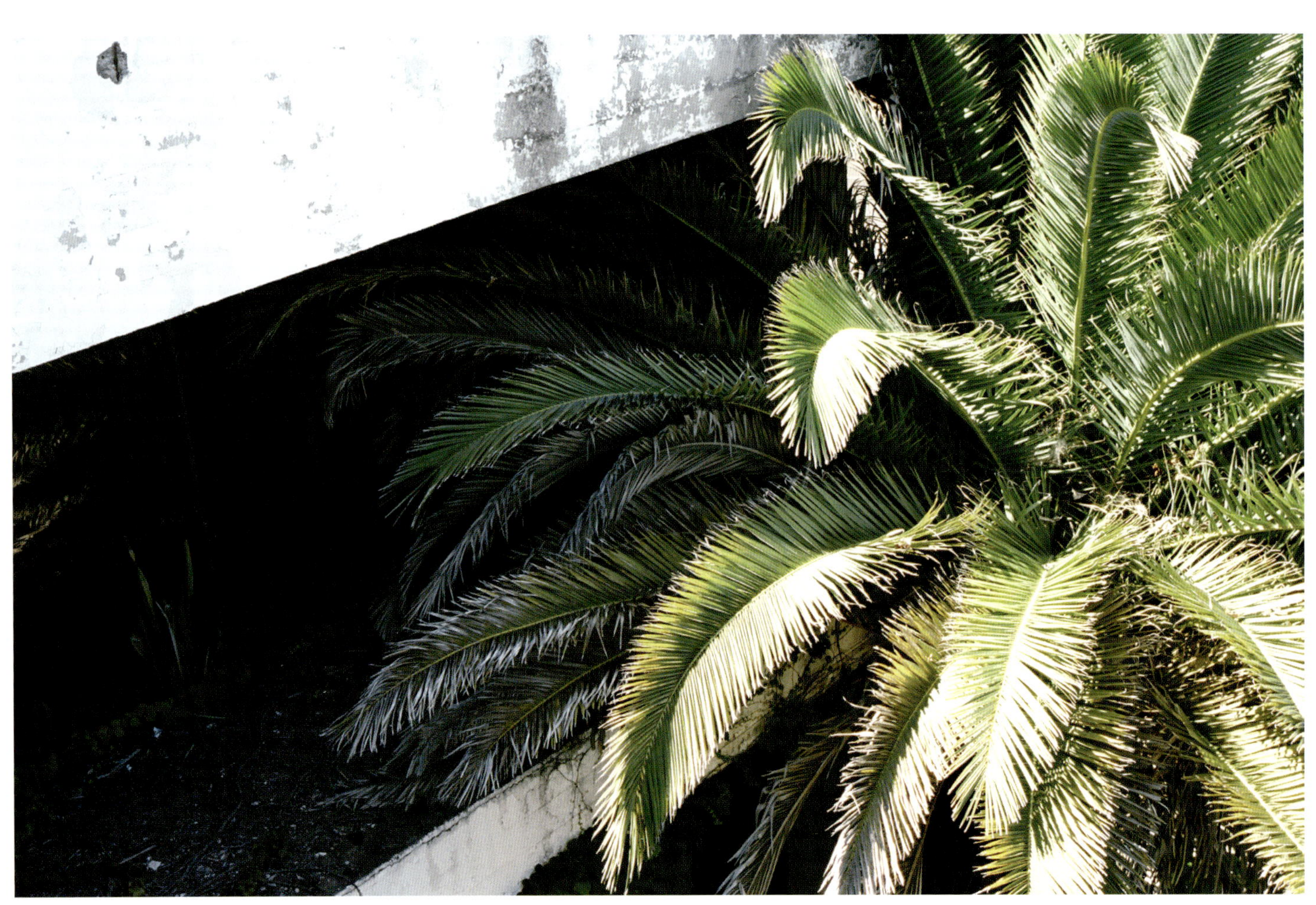

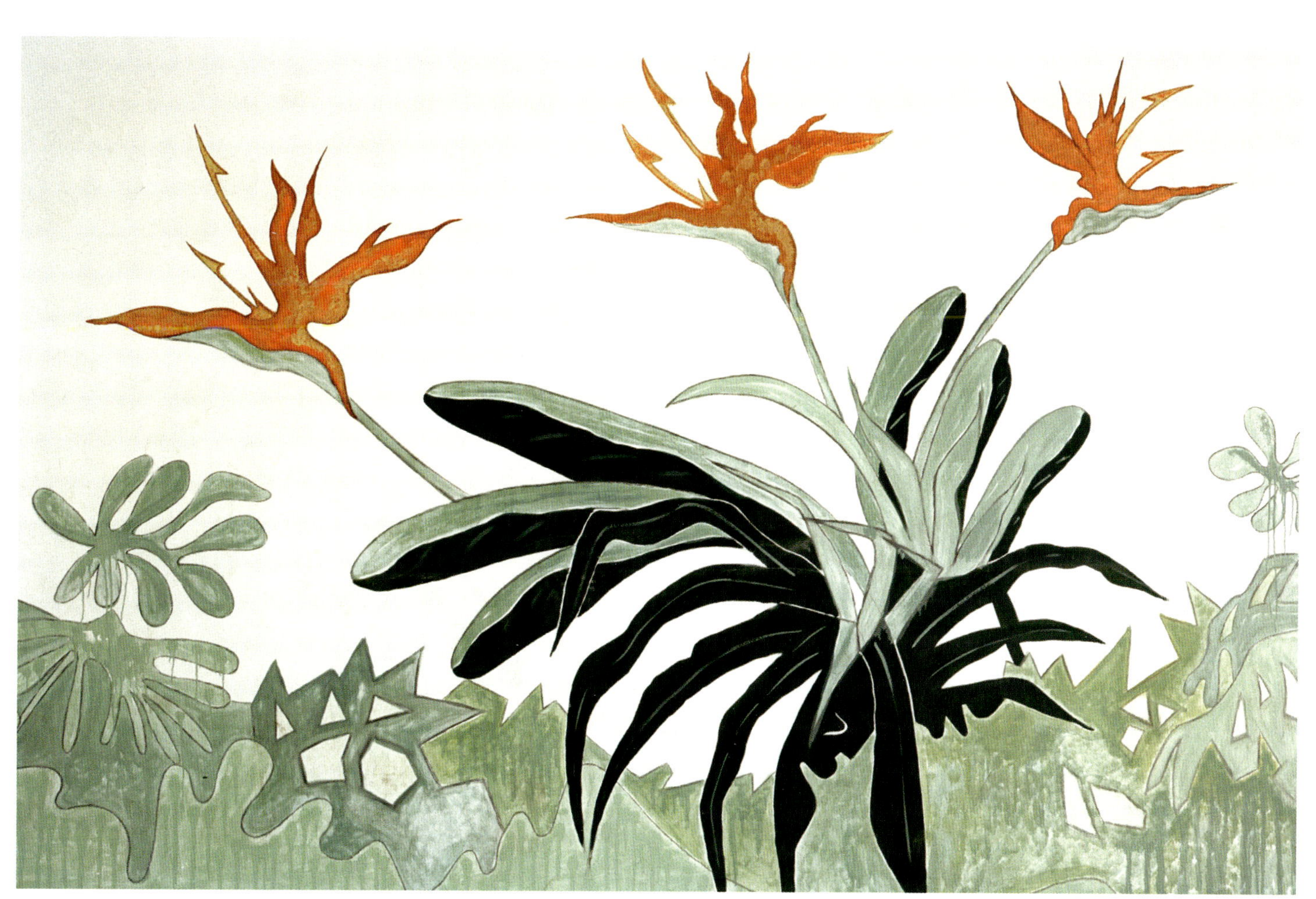

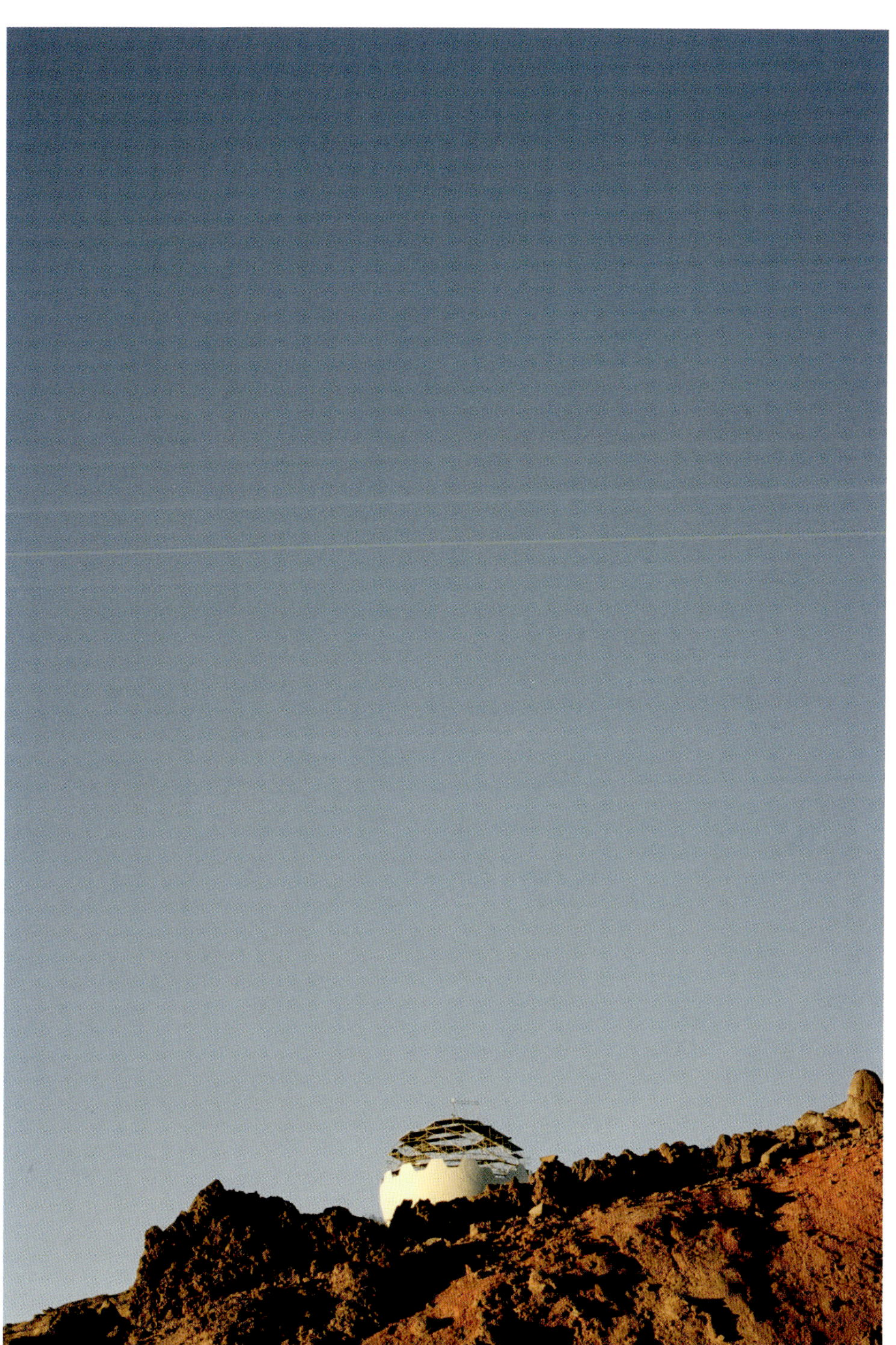

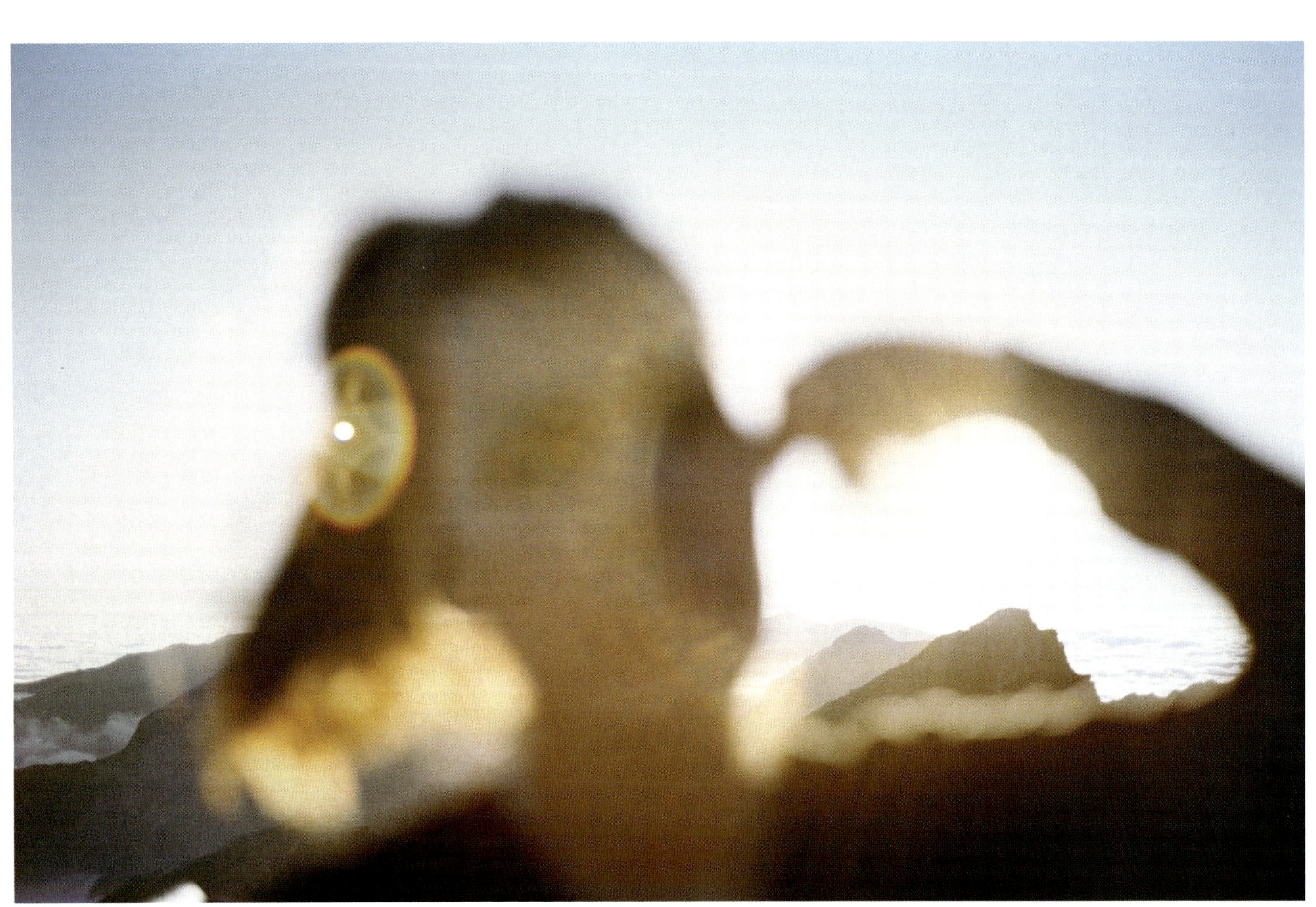

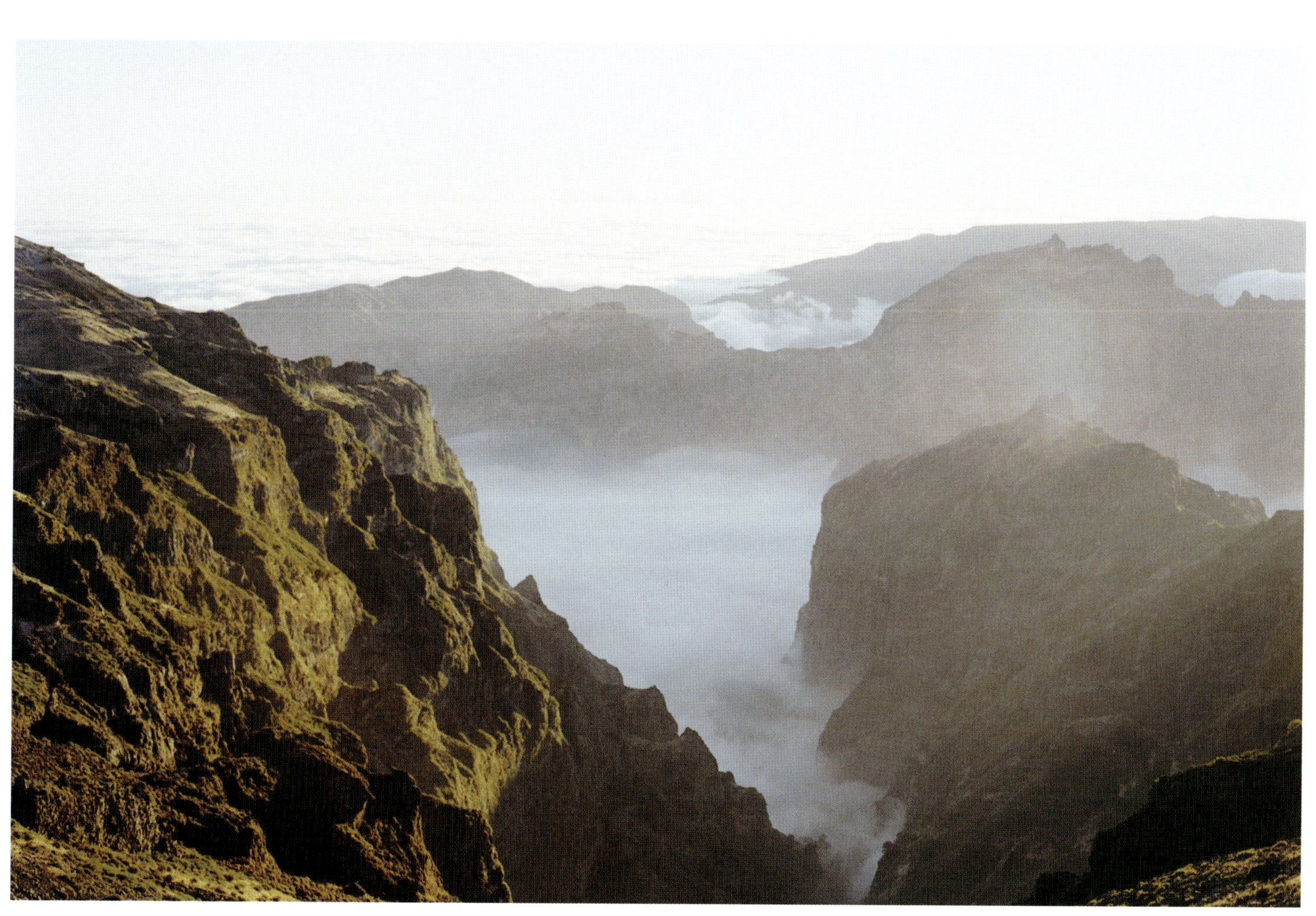

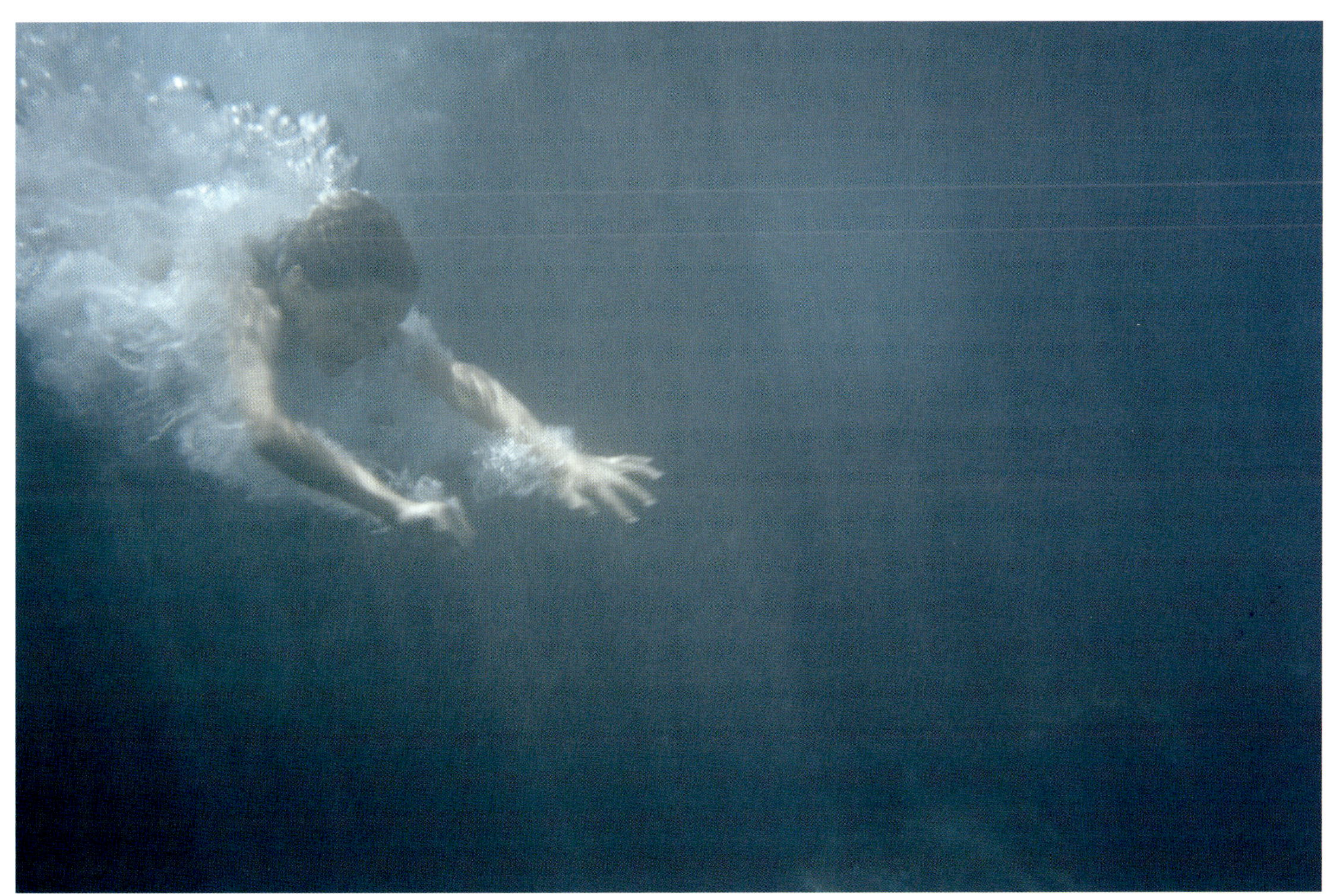

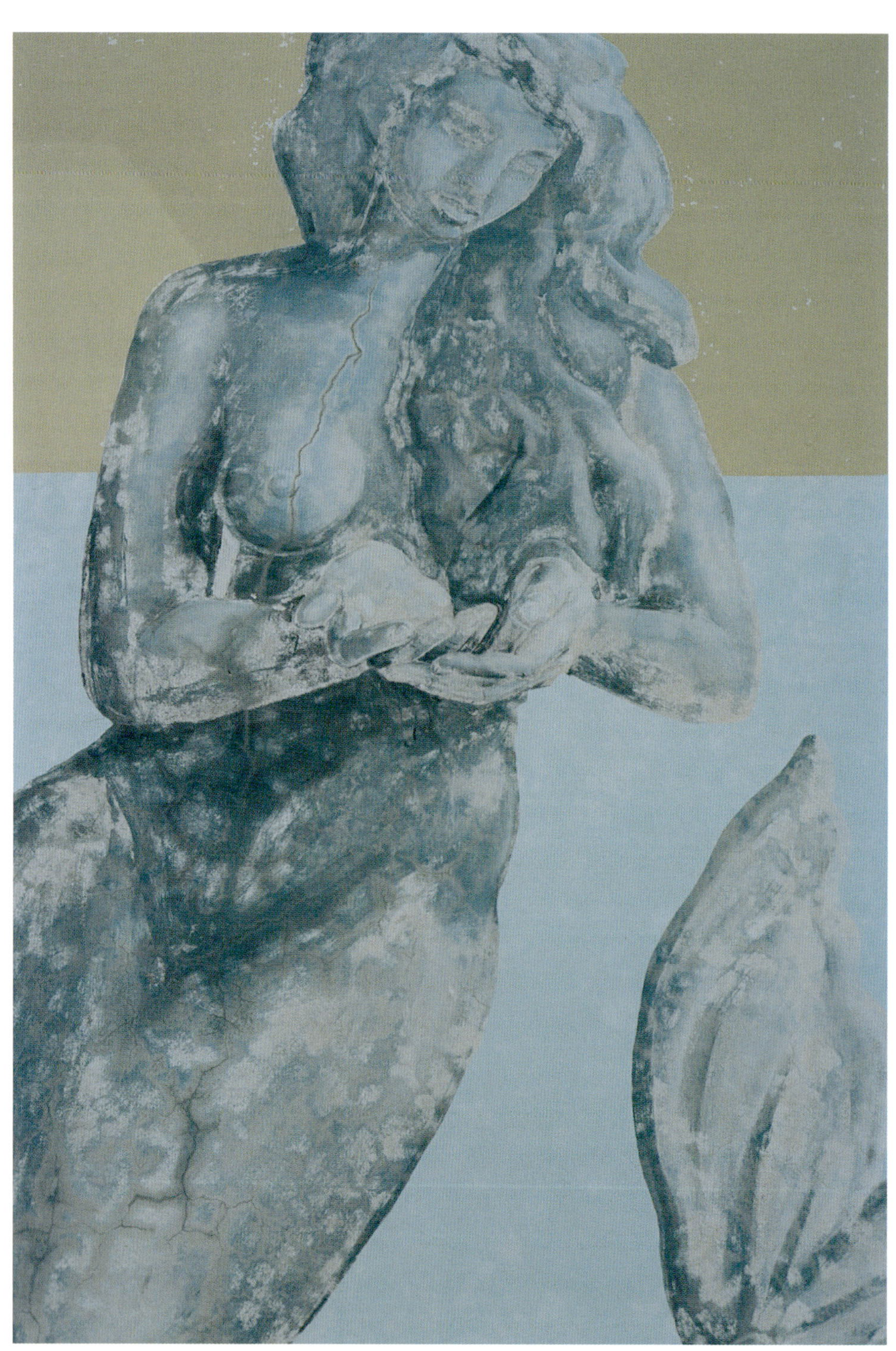

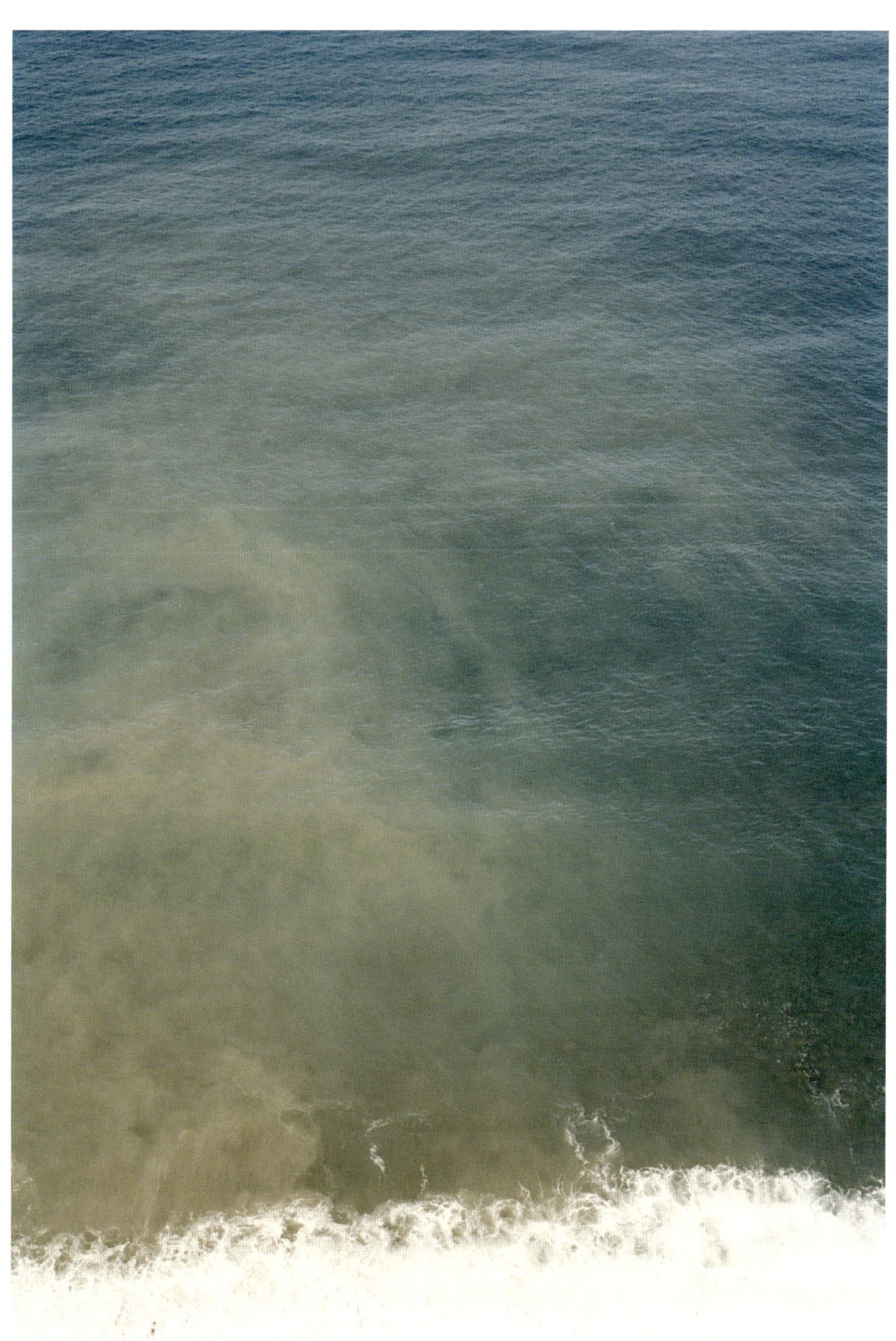

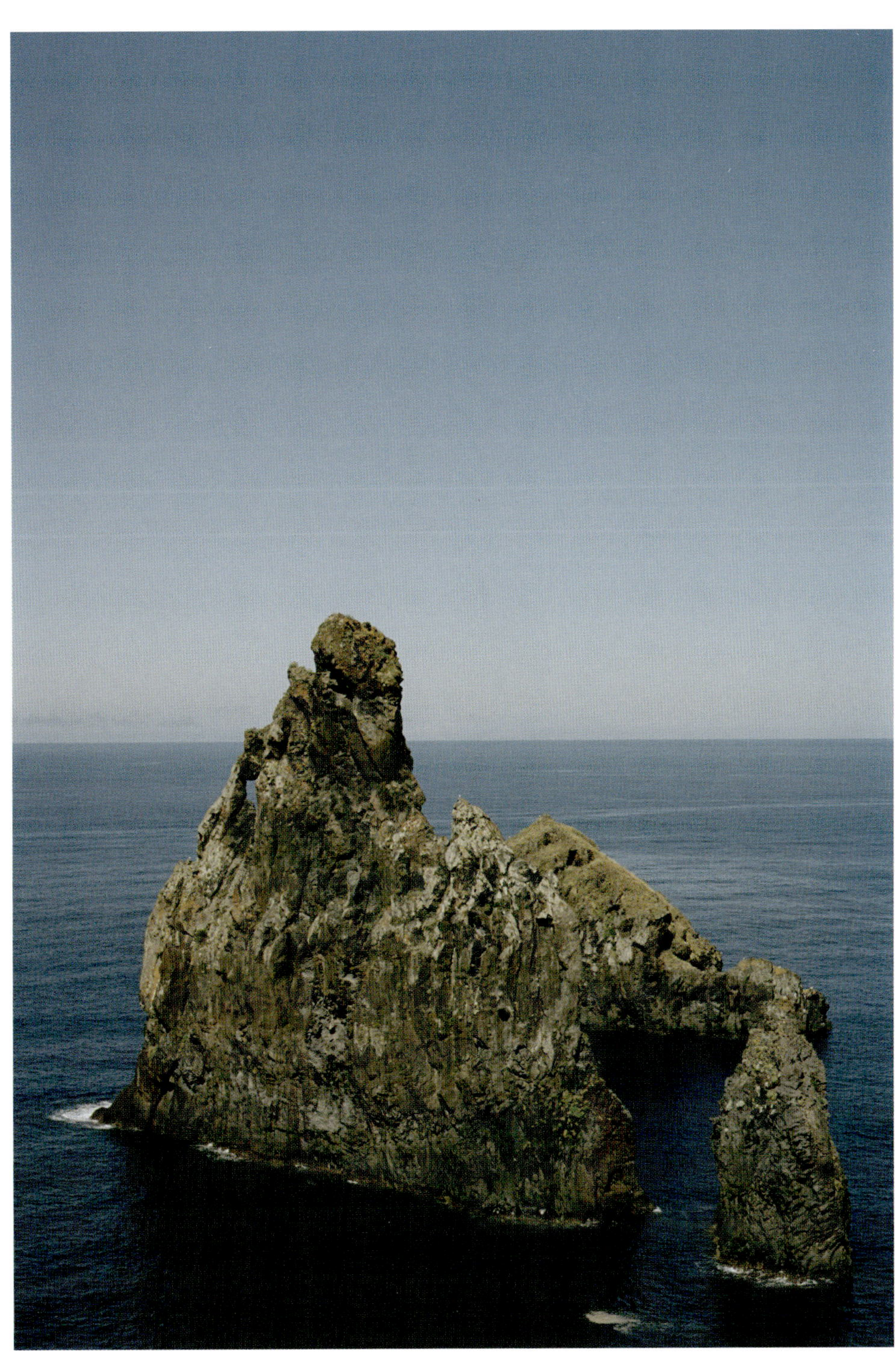

ILHA PEDRO RAMOS
The Spring Press #19

Published by The Spring Press, New York, New York
Ilha is printed in an edition of five hundred copies

ISBN: 978-0-615-82870-1